A LEG
TO
STAND
ON

OLIVER SACKS

A LEG
TO
STAND
ON

PERENNIAL LIBRARY

Harper & Row, Publishers • New York
Cambridge, Philadelphia, San Francisco, Washington
London, Mexico City, São Paulo, Singapore, Sydney

Grateful acknowledgment is made to Oxford University Press for permission to quote from Henry Head's *Studies in Neurology* and to Crown Publishers for permission to quote from Albert Einstein's *Ideas and Opinions,* copyright 1954, © 1982 by Crown Publishers, Inc.

A hardcover edition of this book is published by Summit Books, a division of Simon & Schuster, Inc. It is here reprinted by arrangement with Summit Books, a division of Simon & Schuster, Inc.

First PERENNIAL LIBRARY edition published 1987.

Library of Congress Cataloging-in-Publication Data

Sacks, Oliver W.
    A leg to stand on.

    Reprint. Originally published: New York : Summit Books, c1984.
    1. Sacks, Oliver W. 2. Neurologists—England—Biography. 3. Physically handicapped—England—Biography. I. Title.
RC339.52.S23A35   1987   362.4'3'0924   [B]   86-45685
ISBN 0-06-097082-0 (pbk.)

---

87 88 89 90 91 MPC 10 9 8 7 6 5 4 3 2 1

TO THE MEMORY OF
A.R.LURIA

CONTENTS

PREFACE

Thom Gunn has written powerfully of the "occasions" of poetry. Science has its occasions no less than art: sometimes a dream-metaphor, like Kekulé's snakes; sometimes an analogy, like Newton's apple; sometimes a literal event, the thing-in-itself, which suddenly explodes into unimagined significance, like Archimedes's "Eureka!" in his bath. Every such occasion *is* a eureka or epiphany.

The occasions of medicine are provided by sickness, injury, patients. The occasion of this book was a peculiar injury, or at least an injury with peculiar effects, resulting from an accident on a mountain in Norway. A physician by profession, I had never found myself a patient before, and now I was at once physician and patient. I had imagined my injury (a severe but uncomplicated wound to the muscles and nerves of one leg) to be straightforward and routine, and I was astonished at the profundity of the effects it had: a sort of paralysis and alienation of the leg, reducing it to an "object" which seemed unrelated to me; an abyss of bizarre, and even terrifying, effects. I had no idea what to make of these effects and entertained fears that I might never recover. I found the abyss a horror, and recovery a wonder; and I have since had a deeper sense of the horror and wonder which lurk behind life and which are concealed, as it were, behind the usual surface of health.

Deeply disturbed and puzzled by these singular effects —the central resonances, so to speak, of a peripheral injury—and the absence of adequate reassurance from my own doctor, I wrote to the eminent neuropsychologist A. R. Luria in Moscow. In the course of his reply he wrote: "Such syndromes are perhaps common, but very uncommonly described." When I recovered from my injury and returned to being a doctor, I found that this was indeed the case. Over the years I investigated some hundreds of patients, all with singular disorders of body-image and body-ego which were neurologically determined and essentially similar to my own. I discuss this work and its implications in outline in the last chapter of this book. I hope to publish a detailed monograph on the subject later.

Thus many themes are interwoven here: the specific neuropsychological and existential phenomena associated with my injury and recovery; the business of being a patient and of returning later to the outside world; the complexities of the doctor-patient relationship and the difficulties of dialogue between them, especially in a matter which is puzzling to both; the application of my findings to a large group of patients, and the pondering of their implication and meaning—all this leading, finally, to a critique of current neurological medicine, and to a vision of what may be the neurological medicine of the future.

This last did not come till several years later. Its occasion was a long train-ride from Boston to New York, when I read Henry Head's great *Studies in Neurology* (1920): *his* journey so similar to my own, from the examination of the effects of a cut nerve in himself to the most general concepts of body-image and body-music. My final chapter was written on a mountain in Costa Rica, completing the odyssey begun on that fateful mountain in Norway.

Except in the last chapter the material is not presented systematically. The book may be regarded as a sort of neurological novel or short story, but one which is rooted in personal experience and neurological fact, such as Luria has given us in *The Man with a Shattered World*, and his other "neurographies."

In all this I was greatly assisted and encouraged by Luria, with whom I had the privilege of an intimate correspondence from 1973 until his death in 1977. In the course of our correspondence he wrote: "You are discovering an entirely new field. . . . Please publish your observations. It may do something to alter the 'veterinary' approach to peripheral disorders, and to open the way to a deeper and more human medicine." To the late A. R. Luria, the pioneer of a new and deeper medicine, I dedicate this book in grateful memory.

London & New York
September 1983   O. W. S.

ACKNOWLEDGEMENTS

Since the events of which this book tells, I have—as indicated in the final section—examined the problems of some hundreds of patients with disorders of body-image caused (like mine) by peripheral problems. In this I was greatly encouraged by the late Dr. Arthur Abrahamson, a pioneer in rehabilitation with a rare insight into the problems of such patients, and fortified by his being himself a paraplegic and amputee. I am very grateful to Dr. Henry Fleck, who performed electrical studies on my own damaged leg, and on many other patients whom we studied together. Mrs. P. C. Carolan has been of invaluable assistance in electroencephalographic and evoked-potential studies of many of our patients with strange disturbances of body-image.

I owe a special debt to Mary-Kay Wilmers, who suggested my article "The Leg" and edited it for publication in the *London Review of Books* (June 1982, v. 4 no. 11). This "released" me to write on a subject I had kept silence on for almost eight years, and acted as a catalyst, or "starter," for this book. But to start is one thing, to finish another: I would never have completed this book without the continuing faith, encouragement and sensitive judgment of my editors—Jim Silberman and Ileene Smith of Summit Books.

Medicine always claims that experience is the test of its operations. Plato therefore was right in saying that to become a true doctor, a man must have experienced all the illnesses he hopes to cure and all the accidents and circumstances he is to diagnose. . . . Such a man I would trust. For the rest guide us like the person who paints seas, rocks and harbors while sitting at his table and sails his model of a ship in perfect safety. Throw him into the real thing, and he does not know where to begin.

—*Montaigne,* ESSAYS *3.13*

CHAPTER ONE

THE MOUNTAIN

This world of limitless silences had nothing hospitable; it received the visitor at his own risk, or rather it scarcely even received him, it tolerated his penetration into its fastnesses in a manner that boded no good: it made him aware of the menace of the elemental, a menace not even hostile, but impersonally deadly.

—Thomas Mann, *The Magic Mountain*

Saturday the 24th started overcast and sullen, but there was promise of fine weather later in the day. I could start my climb early, through the low-lying orchards and woods, and by noon, I reckoned, reach the top of the mountain. By then, perhaps, the weather would have cleared, and there would be a magnificent view from the summit—the lower mountains all around me, sweeping down into Hardanger fjørd, and the great fjørd itself visible in its entirety. "Climb" suggests scaling rocks, and ropes. But it was not that sort of climb, simply a steep mountain path. I foresaw no particular problems or difficulties. I was as strong as a bull, in the prime, the pride, the high noon of life. I looked forward to the walk with assurance and pleasure.

I soon got into my stride—a supple swinging stride, which covers ground fast. I had started before dawn, and by half past seven had ascended, perhaps, to 2,000 feet. Already the early mists were beginning to clear. Now came a dark and piney wood, where the going was slower, partly because of knotted roots in the path and partly because I was enchanted by the world of tiny vegetation which sheltered in the wood, and was always stopping to examine a new fern, a moss, a lichen. Even so, I was through the woods by a little after nine, and had come to the great cone which formed the mountain proper and towered above the fjørd to 6,000 feet. To my surprise there was a fence and a gate at this point, and the gate bore a still more surprising notice:

BEWARE OF THE BULL!

in Norwegian, and for those who might not be able to read the words, a rather droll picture of a man being tossed.

I stopped, and scrutinized the picture and scatched my head. A *bull? Up Here?* What would a bull be doing up here? I had not even seen sheep in the pastures and farms down below. Perhaps it was some sort of joke, tacked there by the villagers, or by some previous hiker with an odd sense of humor. Or perhaps there *was* a bull, summering amid a vast mountain pasture, subsisting on the spare grass and scrubby vegetation. Well, enough of speculation. Onwards to the top. The terrain had changed again. It was now very stoney, with enormous boulders here and there; but there was also a light topsoil, muddy in places because it had rained in the night, but with plenty of grass and a few scanty shrubs—fodder enough for an animal which had the whole mountain to graze. The path was much steeper and pretty well marked though, I felt, not much used. It was not exactly a populous part of the world. I had seen no visitors apart from myself, and the villagers, I imagined, were too busy with farming and fishing, and other activities, to go jaunting up the local mountains. All the better. I had the mountain to myself! Onwards, up-wards—though I could not see the top, but I had already ascended, I judged, 3,000 feet, and if the path ahead was simply steep, but not tricky, I could make the top by noon, as I had planned. And so I forged ahead, keeping up a brisk pace despite the gradient, blessing my energy and stamina, and especially my strong legs, trained by years of hard exercise and hard lifting in the gym. Strong quads, strong body, good wind, good stamina—I was grateful to Nature for endowing me well. And if I drove myself to feats-of-strength, and long swims, and long climbs, it was a way of saying "Thank you" to Nature and using to the full the good body she had given me. Around eleven o'clock, when the shifting mists allowed, I had my first glimpses of the mountain top—not so far above me—I *would* make it by noon. There was still a light mist clinging here and there, sometimes shrouding the boulders so that they were difficult to make out. Occasionally a boulder, half seen through the mist, looked almost like a vast crouching animal, and would only reveal its true nature when I came closer. There were ambiguous moments when I would stop in uncertainty, while I descried the shrouded shapes before me. . . . But when it happened, it was not at all ambiguous!

The real Reality was not such a moment, not touched in the least by ambiguity or illusion. I had, indeed, just emerged from the mist, and was walking round a boulder as big as a house, the path curving round it so that I could not see ahead, and it was this inability to see ahead which permitted *the Meeting*. I practically trod on what lay before me—an enormous animal sitting in the path, and indeed totally occupying the path, whose presence had been hidden by the rounded bulk of the rock. It had a huge horned head, a stupendous white body and an enormous mild milk-white face. It sat unmoved by my appearance, exceedingly calm, except that it turned its vast white face up towards me. And in that moment it *changed*, before my eyes, becoming transformed from magnificent to utterly monstrous. The huge white face seemed to swell and swell, and the great bulbous eyes became radiant with malignance. The face grew huger and huger all the time, until I thought it would blot out the Universe. The bull became hideous—hideous beyond belief, hideous in strength, malevolence and cunning. It seemed now to be stamped with the infernal in every feature. It became, first a monster, and now the Devil.

I retained my composure, or a semblance of composure, for a minute, in which, perfectly "naturally," as if turning about at the end of a stroll, I swung in mid-stride through 180 degrees, and deftly, daintily, began my descent. But then—oh horrible!—my nerve suddenly broke, dread overwhelmed me, and I ran for dear life—ran madly, blindly, down the steep, muddy, slippery path, lost here and there in patches of mist. Blind, mad panic!—there is nothing worse in the world, nothing worse—and nothing more *dangerous*. I cannot say exactly what happened. In my plunging flight down the treacherous path I must have mis-stepped—stepped on to a loose rock, or into mid-air. It is as if there is a moment missing from my memory—there is "before" and "after," but no "in-between." One moment I was running like a madman, conscious of heavy panting and heavy thudding footsteps, unsure whether they came from the bull or from me, and the next I was lying at the bottom of a short sharp cliff of rock, with my left leg twisted grotesquely beneath me, and in my knee such a pain as I had never, ever known. To be full of strength and vigor one moment and virtually helpless the next, in the pink and pride of health one moment and a cripple the next, with all one's powers and faculties one moment and without them the next—such a change, such suddenness, is difficult to comprehend, and the mind casts about for explanations.

I had encountered this phenomenon in others—in my patients who had been suddenly stricken or injured, and now I was to encounter it in myself. My first thought was this: that there had been an accident, and that *someone I knew* had been seriously injured. Later, it dawned on me that the victim was myself; but with this came the feeling that it was not really serious. To show that it was not serious, I got to my feet, or rather I *tried* to, but I collapsed in the process, because the left leg was totally limp and flail, and gave way beneath me like a piece of spaghetti. It could not support any weight at all, but just buckled beneath me, buckled backwards at the knee, making me yell with pain. But it was much less the pain that so horribly frightened me than the flimsy, toneless giving-way of the knee and my absolute impotence to prevent or control it—and the apparent paralysis of the leg. And then, the horror, so overwhelming for a moment, disappeared in face of a "professional attitude."

"OK, Doctor," I said to myself, "would you kindly examine the leg?"

Very professionally, and impersonally, and not at all tenderly, as if I were a surgeon examining "a case," I took the leg and examined it—feeling it, moving it this way and that. I murmured my findings aloud as I did so, as if for a class of students:

"No movement at the knee, gentlemen, no movement at the hip. . . . You will observe that the entire quadriceps has been torn from the patella. But though it has torn loose, it has not retracted—it is wholly toneless, which might suggest nerve injury as well. The patella has lost its major attachment, and can be flipped around—so!—like a ball-bearing. It is readily dislocated—there is nothing to hold it. As for the knee itself—" and here I illustrated each point as I made it—"we find abnormal motility, a quite pathological range of motion. It can be flexed without any resistance at all—" here I manually flexed the heel to the buttock—"and can also be hyperextended, with no apparent dislocation"—both movements, which I illustrated, caused me to scream. "Yes, gentlemen," I concluded, summarizing my findings, "a fascinating case! A complete rupture of the quadriceps tendon. Muscle paralyzed and atonic—probably nerve-injury. Unstable knee-joint—seems to dislocate backwards. Probably ripped out the cruciate ligaments. Can't really tell about bone injury—but there could easily be one or more fractures. Considerable swelling, probably tissue and joint fluid, but tearing of blood vessels can't be excluded."

I turned with a pleased smile to my invisible audience, as if awaiting a round of applause. And then, suddenly, the "professional" attitude and *persona* broke down, and I realized that this "fascinating case" was *me—me myself*, fearfully disabled, and quite likely to die. The leg was utterly useless—far more so than if it had been broken. I was entirely alone, near the top of a mountain, in a desolate and sparsely populated part of the world. My whereabouts were known to nobody. This frightened me more than anything else. I could die where I lay, and nobody would know it.

Never had I felt so alone, so lost, so forlorn, so utterly beyond the pale of help. It hadn't occurred to me till then how terrifyingly and seriously alone I was. I had not felt "alone" when I was romping up the mountain (I never do when I am enjoying myself). I had not felt alone when I was examining my injury (I saw now what a comfort the imagined "class" was). But now, all of a sudden, the fearful sense of my aloneness rushed in upon me. I remembered that someone had told me, a few days before, of "a fool of an Englishman" who had climbed this very mountain, alone, two years before, and had been found a week later dead from exposure, having broken both his legs. It was at an altitude, and latitude, where the temperature sinks well below freezing at night, even in August. I had to be found by nightfall or I should never survive. I had to get lower, if I possibly could, because then at least there was a chance of my being seen. I even entertained hopes, now I came to consider things, that I might be able to descend the entire mountain, with a bum leg, by myself; and it was not till much later that I realized how this, above all, was a comforting delusion. Yet, if I pulled myself together, did what I could, there was a sporting chance that I would make it yet.

I suddenly found myself very calm and composed. First of all, I had to address myself to the leg. I had discovered that while any movement at the knee was agonizing, and indeed, literally, physiologically, shocking, I was fairly comfortable when the leg lay flat and supported on the ground. But having no bone or "inner structure" to hold it, it had no protection against helpless passive movements at the knee, as might be caused by any unevenness in the ground. So, clearly, it needed an outer structure, or splint.

And here one of my idiosyncrasies came to my aid. Habit, more than anything else, made me carry an umbrella under all conditions, and it seemed natural enough, or purely automatic, that when I went for a walk in bad weather (even up a mountain over a mile high), I should take my stout and trusty umbrella with me. Besides, it had been useful as a walking stick on the way up. And now it found its finest moment—in splinting my leg—and without such a splint I could scarcely have moved. I snapped off the handle and tore my anorak in two. The length of the umbrella was just right—the heavy shaft almost matched the length of my leg—and I lashed it in place with strong strips of anorak, sufficiently firmly to prevent a helpless flailing of the knee, but not so tightly as to impede circulation. By now about twenty minutes had elapsed since my injury, or possibly less. Could all this have occurred in so short a time? I looked at my watch to see if it had stopped, but the second hand was going round with perfect regularity. *Its* time, abstract, impersonal, chronological, had no relation to my time—*my* time which consisted solely of personal moments, life-moments, crucial moments. As I looked at the dial, I matched, in imagination, the movement of the hands, going steadily round and round—the relentless regularity of the sun in the heavens —with my own uncertain descent of the mountain. I could not think of hurrying—that would exhaust me. I could not think of dawdling—that would be worse. I had to find the right pace, and steadily keep it up.

I found myself now gratefully taking note of my assets and resources, where before I could only take note of the injury. Mercifully, then, I had not torn an artery, or major vessel, internally, for there was only a little swelling round the knee and no real coolness or discoloration of the leg. The quadriceps was apparently paralyzed, it was true— but I made no further neurological examination. I had not fractured my spine or my skull in my fall. And—God be praised!—I had three good limbs, and the energy and strength to put up a good fight. And, by God, I would! This would be the fight of my life—the fight of one's life which is the fight *for* life.

I could not hurry—I could only hope. But my hopes would be extinguished if I were not found by nightfall. Again I looked at my watch, as I was to do many anxious times again in the hours that followed. At these latitudes it would be a rather lengthy evening and dusk, starting around 6 and gradually getting darker and cooler. By 7:30 it would be quite cool, and difficult to see. I had to be found by about 8, at the latest. By 8:30 it would be pitch-black— impossible to see and impossible to proceed. And though by strenuous exercise I might, just conceivably, last through the night, the chances were distinctly, indeed heavily, against it. I thought, for a moment, of Tolstoy's *Master & Man*—but there were not two of us to keep each other warm. If only I had had a companion with me! The thought suddenly came to me once again, in the words from the Bible not read since childhood, and not consciously recollected, or brought to mind, at all: "Two are better than one . . . for if they fall, the one will lift up his fellow; but woe to him that is alone when he falleth, for he hath not another to help him up." And, following immediately upon this, came a sudden memory, eidetically clear, of a small animal I had seen in the road, with a broken back, hoisting its paralyzed hindlegs along. Now I felt exactly like that creature. The sense of my humanity as something apart, something above animality and mortality—this too disappeared at that moment, and again the words of Ecclesiastes came to my mind: "For that which befalleth the sons of men befalleth beasts; as the one dieth, so dieth the other . . . so that a man hath no pre-eminence above a beast."

While splinting my leg, and keeping myself busy, I had again "forgotten" that death lay in wait. Now, once again, it took the Preacher to remind me. "But," I cried inside myself, "the instinct of life is strong within me. I want to live—and, with luck, I may still do so. I don't think it is yet my time to die." Again the Preacher answered, neutral, non-committal: "To everything there is a season, and a time to every purpose under the heaven. A time to be born, and a time to die; a time . . ." This strange, profound emotionless clarity, neither cold, nor warm, neither severe nor indulgent, but utterly, beautifully, terribly *truthful*, I had encountered in others, especially in patients, who were facing death and did not conceal the truth from themselves; I had marvelled, though in a way uncomprehendingly, at the simple ending of *Hadji Murad*—how, when Murad has been fatally shot, "images without feelings" stream through his mind; but now, for the first time, I encountered this—in myself.

These images, and words, and passionless feelings did not, as they say, go through my head "in a flash." They took their time—several minutes at least—the time they would have taken in reality, not in a dream; they were meditations, which did not hurry at all—but neither did they distract me in the least from my tasks. Nobody looking on (so to speak) would have seen me "musing," would have seen any pause. On the contrary, they would have been impressed by my brisk and workmanlike appearance and behavior, by the quick and efficient way in which I splinted my leg, made a brief check of everything, and set off downhill.

And so I proceeded, using a mode of travel I had never used before—roughly speaking, gluteal and tripedal. That is to say, I slid down on my backside, heaving or rowing myself with my arms and using my good leg for steering and, when needed for braking, with the splinted, flail leg hanging nervelessly before me. I did not have to think out this unusual, unprecedented, and—one might think—unnatural way of moving. I did it without thinking, and very soon got accustomed to it. And anyone seeing me rowing swiftly and powerfully down the slopes would have said, "Ah, he's an old hand at it. It's second nature to him."

So the legless don't need to be *taught* to use crutches: it comes "unthinkingly" and "naturally," as if the person had been practicing it, in secret, all his life. The organism, the nervous system, has an immense repertoire of "trick movements" and "back-ups" of every kind—completely automatic strategies, which are held "in reserve." We would have no idea of the resources which exist *in potentia*, if we did not see them called forth as needed.

So it happened with me. It was a reasonably efficient mode of progress, as long as the path descended continually, and evenly, and not too steeply. If it was not even, the left leg would tend to catch on irregularities of all sorts —it seemed curiously inept at avoiding these—and I cursed it out several times for being "stupid" or "senseless." I found, indeed, that whenever the terrain became difficult, I had to keep an eye on this not only powerless but stupid leg. Most frightening of all were those sections of the path which were too slippery or too steep, because it was difficult not to slide down almost uncontrollably, ending with a lurch or a crash which agonizingly buckled the knee and exposed the limitations of my improvised splint.

It occurred to me at one point, after a particularly sickening crash, to cry for help, and I did so, lustily, with Gargantuan yells, which seemed to echo and resound from one peak to another. The sudden sound in the silence startled and scared me; and then I had a sudden fear that it might startle the bull, which I had completely forgotten. I had a frightened vision of the animal, now furiously re-aroused, charging down the path to toss me or crush me. Trembling with terror, and with immense effort and pain, I managed to heave myself off the path until I was hidden behind a boulder. Here I remained for about ten minutes, until the continuing silence reassured me and I was able to crawl out and continue my descent. I could not decide whether it had been foolish and provocative to yell, or whether my folly lay rather in fearing to yell. I decided, in any event, not to yell again; and whenever the impulse seized me I held my tongue, remembering that I was still in the bull's domain, where perhaps he maintained a sharp-eared dominion; and I would further say to myself, for good measure, "Why shout? Save your breath. You're the only human being in hundreds of square miles." And so I descended in absolute silence, not even daring to whistle aloud for everywhere now I felt the bull listening. I even tried to mute the sound of my breathing. And so the hours passed, silently, slithering. . . .

At about 1:30—I had been travelling two hours—I came again to the swollen stream with stepping-stones that I had hesitated to cross even when climbing up, with both legs. Clearly, I could not "row" myself through this. I had therefore to turn over and "walk" on rigidly outstretched arms—and even so my head was only just out of the water. The water was fast-flowing, turbulent and glacially cold, and my left leg, dropping downwards, unsupported, out of control, was violently jarred by stones on the bottom, and sometimes blown like a flag sideways at a right-angle to my trunk. My hip seemed almost as loose as my knee, but it caused me no pain—unlike my knee which, excruciatingly, was buckled and dislocated as I crossed the stream. Several times I felt my consciousness ebbing and feared I would faint and drown in the stream; and I ordered myself to hold on, with strong language and threats.

"Hold on, you fool! Hold on for dear life! I'll *kill* you if you let go—and don't you forget it!"

I half collapsed when finally I made the other side, shuddering with cold, and pain and shock. I felt exhausted, prostrated, at the end of my strength, and I lay stunned, motionless, for a couple of minutes. Then, somehow my exhaustion became a sort of tiredness, an extraordinarily comfortable, delicious languor.

"How nice it is here," I thought to myself. "Why not a little rest—a nap maybe?"

The apparent sound of this soft, insinuating, inner voice suddenly woke me, sobered me and filled me with alarm. It was not "a nice place" to rest and nap. The suggestion was lethal and filled me with horror, but I was lulled by its soft, seductive tones.

"No," I said fiercely to myself. "This is Death speaking—and in its sweetest, deadliest Siren-voice. Don't listen to it now! Don't listen to it ever! You've got to go on whether you like it or not. You can't rest here—you can't rest anywhere. You must find a pace you can keep up, and go on steadily."

This good voice, this "life" voice, braced and resolved me. My trembling stopped and my faltering too. I got going once more, and didn't falter again.

There came to my aid now melody, rhythm and music (what Kant calls the "quickening" art). Before crossing the stream, I had *muscled* myself along—moving by main force, with my very strong arms. Now, so to speak, I was *musicked* along. I did not contrive this. It happened to me. I fell into a rhythm, guided by a sort of marching or rowing song, sometimes the Volga Boatmen's Song, sometimes a monotonous chant of my own, accompanied by these words *"Ohne Haste, ohne Rast! Ohne Haste, ohne Rast!"* ("Without haste, without rest"), with a strong heave on every *Haste* and *Rast*. Never had Goethe's words been put to better use! Now, I no longer had to think about going too fast or too slow. I got into the music, got into the swing, and this ensured that my tempo was right. I found myself perfectly co-ordinated by the rhythm—or perhaps sub-ordinated would be a better term: the musical beat was generated within me, and all my muscles responded obediently—all save those in my left leg which seemed silent—or mute? Does not Nietzsche say that when listen-ing to music, we "listen with our muscles?" I was reminded of my rowing days in College, how the eight of us would respond as one man to the beat, a sort of muscle-orchestra conducted by the cox.

Somehow, with this "music," it felt much less like a grim anxious struggle. There was even a certain primitive exuberance, such as Pavlov called "muscular gladness." And now, further, to gladden me more, the sun burst from behind the clouds, massaged me with warmth and soon dried me off. And with all this, and perhaps other things, I found my internal weather was most happily changed.

It was only after chanting the song in a resonant and resounding bass for some time that I suddenly realized that I had forgotten the bull. Or, more accurately, I had for-gotten my fear—partly seeing that it was no longer appro-priate, partly that it had been absurd in the first place. I had no room now for this fear, or for any other fear, be-cause I was filled to the brim with music. And even when it was not literally (audibly) music, there was the music of my muscle-orchestra playing—"the silent music of the body," in Harvey's lovely phrase. With this playing, the musicality of my motion, I myself became the music—"You are the music, while the music lasts." A creature of muscle, motion and music, all inseparable and in unison with each other—except for that unstrung part of me, that poor broken instrument which could not join in and lay motionless and mute without tone or tune.

As a child I had once had a violin which got brutally smashed in an accident. I felt for my leg, now, as I felt long ago for that poor broken fiddle. Admixed with my happiness and renewal of spirit, with the quickening music I felt in myself, was a new and sharper and most poignant sense of loss for that broken musical instrument which had once been my leg. When will it recover, I thought to myself? When will it sound its own tune again? When will it rejoin the joyous music of the body? Oh, *when*?

By two o'clock the clouds had cleared sufficiently for me to get a magnificent view of the fjørd beneath me, and of the tiny village I had left nine hours before. I could see the old church, where I had heard Mozart's great Mass in C Minor the previous evening. I could almost see—no, I *could* see—individual figures in the street. Was the air abnormally, uncannily, clear? Or was there some abnormal clarity in my perceptions? I thought of a dream related by Leibniz, in which he found himself at a great height over-looking the world—with provinces, towns, lakes, fields, villages, hamlets, all spread beneath him. If he wished to see a single person—a peasant tilling, an old woman wash-ing clothes—he had only to direct and concentrate his gaze: "I needed no telescope except my attention." And so it was with me: an anguish of yearning sharpened my eyes, a violent need to see my fellow-men and, even more, to be seen by them. Never had they seemed dearer, or more re-mote. I felt so close, watching them as through a powerful telescope, and yet utterly removed, not part of their world.

If only I had a flag, or a flare—a rifle, a carrier-pigeon, a radio-transmitter! If only I could give a truly Gargantuan yell—one which would be heard ten miles away! For how could they know that here was a fellow-creature, a crippled human being, fighting for his life 5,000 feet above them? I was within sight of my rescuers, and yet I would probably die. There was something impersonal, or universal, in my feeling. I would not have cried "Save *me*, Oliver Sacks!" but "Save this hurt living creature! Save *life!*," the mute plea I know so well from my patients—the plea of *all* life facing the abyss, if it be strongly, vividly, rightly alive.

An hour passed, and another, and another, under a glorious cloudless sky, the sun blazing pale-golden with a pure Arctic light. It was an afternoon of peculiar splendor, earth and air conspiring in beauty, radiant, tranquil, suffused in serenity. As the blue and golden hours passed, I continued steadily on my downward trek, which had become so smooth, so void of difficulties, that my mind could move free of the ties of the present. My mood changed again, although I was to realize this only later. Long-forgotten memories, all happy, came unbidden to my mind: memories, first, of summer afternoons, tinged with a sunnniness which was also happiness and blessed- ness—sun-warmed afternoons with my family and friends, summer afternoons going back into earliest childhood Hundreds of memories would pass through my mind, in the space between one boulder and the next, and yet each was rich, simple, ample, complete, and conveyed no sense of being hurried through.

Nor was it a flitting of faces and voices. Entire scenes were re-lived, entire conversations re-played, without the least abreviation. The very earliest memories were all of our garden—our big old garden in London, as it used to be before the war. I cried with joy and tears as I saw it— our garden with its dear old iron railings intact, the lawn vast and smooth, just cut and rolled (the huge old roller there in a corner); the orange-striped hammock with cushions bigger than myself, in which I loved to roll and swing for hours; and—joy of my heart—the enormous sunflowers, whose vast inflorescences fascinated me endlessly and showed me at five the Pythagorean mystery of the world. (For it was then, in the summer of 1938, that I discovered that the whorled florets were multiples of prime numbers, and I had such a vision of the order and beauty of the world as was to be a prototype of every scientific wonder and joy I was later to experience.) All of these thoughts and images, involuntarily summoned and streaming through my mind, were essentially happy, and essentially grateful. And it was only later that I said to myself "What is this mood?" and realized that it was a preparation for death. "Let your last thinks all be thanks," as Auden says.

At about six, rather suddenly, I noticed that the shadows were longer, and that the sun was no longer high in the heavens. Some part of me, Joshua-like, had thought to hold the sun in mid-course, to prolong to eternity the gold and azure afternoon. Now, abruptly, I saw that it was evening, and that in an hour, more or less, the sun would set.

It was not long after this that I came to a long transverse ridge commanding an unobstructed view of the village and fjørd. I had attained this ridge at about ten in the morning: it had been about half-way between the gate and the point where I fell. Thus what had taken me little more than an hour to climb, had taken me, crippled, nearly seven hours to descend. I saw how grossly, how optimistically, I had miscalculated everything—comparing my "rowing" to striding, when it was, I could now see, six times as slow. How could I have imagined that one was half as fast as the other, and that the ascent from the relatively warm and populous low-lying farmland, which had taken four hours or so, could be retraced in just twice that time, bringing me within range of the highest farmhouse by dusk or nightfall. I had hugged to myself, like a warm comforter, in the long hours of my journey—interspersed with my exalted but not cozy thoughts—a warm sweet vision of the waiting farmhouse, glowing softly like a Dutch interior, with a dumpy, motherly farmwife who would feed me and revive me with love and warm milk, while her husband, a dour giant, went to the village for help. I had been secretly sustained by this vision throughout the interminable hours of my descent, and now it vanished, suddenly, like a candle blown out, on the chill clarity of that high transverse ridge.

I could see now, what had been shrouded in mists on the way up in the morning, how far away, unattainably far, the village still was. And yet, though hope had just expired and died, I took comfort from seeing the village, and especially the church, gilded, or rather crimsoned now, in the long evening light. I could see straggling worshippers on their way to evening service and had the strangest persuasion that the service was for me. It came to me once more, and overwhelmingly, how I had sat in that church only the evening before, and heard the C minor mass, and so powerful was the memory that I could actually hear it in my ears—hear it with such vividness that I wondered, for a long second, whether it was again being sung below, and wafted up to me, miraculously, by some trick of the air. As I listened, profoundly moved, with tears on my face, I suddenly realized that it was not the mass that I was hearing—no, not the mass, but the Requiem instead. My mind, my unconscious, had switched one for the other. Or was it—again that uncanny acoustic illusion—was it that they *were* singing the Requiem, down there for me?

Shortly after seven the sun disappeared, seeming to draw, as it did so, all color and warmth from the world. There were none of the lingering effulgencies of a more temperate sunset—this was a simpler, sterner, more Arctic phenomenon. The air was suddenly grayer, and colder, and the grayness and coldness seemed to penetrate right to my marrow.

The silence had become intense. I could no longer hear any sounds about me. *I could no longer hear myself.* Everything seemed embedded in silence. There were odd periods when I thought I was dead, when the immense calm became the calm of death. Things had ceased to happen. There was no happening any more. This must be the beginning of the end.

Suddenly, incredibly, I heard a shout, a long yodelling call which seemed very close to me. I turned, and saw a man and a boy standing on a rock, a little above me, and not ten yards from the path, their figures silhouetted against the darkening dusk. I never even saw my rescuers before they saw me. I think, in those last dark minutes, that my eyes had been fixed on the dim path before me, or had perhaps been staring unseeing into space—they had ceased to be on the look-out, constantly roving and scanning, as they had been at all times in the course of the day. I think, indeed, that I had become almost totally unaware of the environment, having, at some level, given up all thoughts of rescue and life, so that rescue, when it came, came from nowhere, a miracle, a grace, at the very last moment. In another few minutes it would have been too dark to see. The man who yodelled was just lowering a gun, and the youth by his side was similarly armed. They ran down towards me, I needed no words to explain my condition. I hugged them both, I kissed them—these bearers of life. I stammered out, in broken Norwegian, what had happened on the heights, and what I could not put into words I drew in the dust.

The two of them laughed at my picture of the bull. They were full of humor, these two, and as they laughed I laughed too—and suddenly, with the laughter, the tragic tension exploded, and I felt vividly and, so to speak, comically alive once again. I thought I had had every emotion on the heights, but—it now occurred to me—I hadn't laughed once. Now I couldn't stop laughing—the laughter of relief, and the laughter of love, that deep-down laughter which comes from the center of one's being. The silence was exploded, that quite deathly silence which had seized me, as in a spell, those last minutes.

The men were reindeer hunters, father and son, who had pitched camp nearby. Hearing a noise outside, a movement in the undergrowth, they had come out cautiously with their rifles at the ready, their minds on the game they might bag, and when they peered over the rock they saw that their game was me.

The huntsman gave me some aquavit from a flask—the burning liquid was indeed the "water of life." "Don't worry," he said, "I go down to the village. I will be back within two hours. My son will stay with you. You're safe and sound—and the bull won't come here!"

From the moment of my rescue my memories become less vivid, less charged. I was in others' hands now and had no more responsibility to act, or feel. I said very little to the boy, but though we hardly spoke I found great comfort in his presence. Occasionally he would light me a cigarette—or pass me the aquavit his father had left. I had the deepest sense of security and warmth. I fell asleep.

It was less than two hours before a posse of stout villagers arrived carrying a litter—on to which they loaded me, with considerable difficulty. The flailing leg, which had lain silent and unnoticed for so long, objected loudly, but they carried me gently, rhythmically, down the steep mountain trail. At the gate—the gate, whose warning sign I had ignored!—I was transferred on to a sort of mountain tractor. As it jogged slowly downhill—first through the woods, and then through orchards and farms—the men sang softly among themselves, and passed the aquavit around. One of them gave me a pipe to smoke. I was back —God be praised!—in the good world of men.

CHAPTER TWO

BECOMING A PATIENT

What's become of man's great extent and proportion, when himself shrinks himself and consumes himself to a handful of dust? . . . A sick bed is a grave. . . . Here the head lies as low as the foot—miserable and (though common to all) inhuman posture! . . . I cannot rise out of my bed till the physician enable me, nay I cannot tell that I am able to rise till he tell me so. I do nothing, I know nothing, of myself.

—John Donne, *Devotions*

"And so I was saved—and that's the end of the story." I had been through what I thought would be "my last day on earth," with all the passions and thoughts attendant on this, and now—to my incredulous surprise and joy I found myself very much back on earth, with a stupid broken leg into the bargain. From this point until—well, you will hear!—there ceased, in a sense, to be any "story," or any particular "mood" to give tension and connection to the days that followed. And thus it is difficult to write about them—difficult even to remember them vividly. I had observed this on the Mountain, as soon as I had the certainty, the comfort, the assurance, of being safe—a sudden relinquishment, and perhaps exhaustion, of feeling—for profound and passionate feelings were no longer needed, no longer suited to my changed and, so to speak, prosaic position—so different from the tragedy, comedy and poetry of the Mountain. I had returned to the prose, the everydayness, and, yes, the pettiness of the world.

And yet, I cannot end my story here, for there was to be another story or, perhaps, another act in the same strange complex drama, which I found utterly surprising and unexpected at the time and almost beyond my comprehension or belief. I thought of these, for a time, as two separate stories, and it was only gradually that I came to see that they were essentially connected. But in terms of feeling at the time the next four days were somewhat dull—even though they included a massive and essential operation, the operation which links the two—and I can recall only certain high points, and low points, which stood out from the overall flatness of that time.

I was taken to the local doctor—himself a red-faced son of the soil, with a practice covering a hundred square miles of the rugged mountain and fjørd country around—who made a swift and decisive, yet unhurried, examination.

"You've torn the quadriceps off," he said. "I don't know what else. You will have to be taken to hospital."

He arranged an ambulance, and alerted the nearest hospital, about sixty miles away, at Odda.

Shortly after I had been settled in the little ward at Odda—it was a cottage hospital, with only a dozen beds or so, and simple facilities to cover the common needs of the community—the nurse came in, a lovely creature, though indefinably rigid and graceless in her movements.

I asked her name.

"Nurse Solveig," she replied, stiffly.

"Solveig?" I exclaimed. "That makes me think of *Peer Gynt!*"

"*Nurse* Solveig, please—my name doesn't matter. And now, be so kind, please, and turn over. I have to insert the rectal thermometer."

"Nurse Solveig," I replied, "can't you take my temperature by mouth? I am in a good deal of pain, and my damn knee will go out on me if I try to turn over."

"I cannot help that," she answered coldly. "I have my orders, and I have to follow them. It is a hospital rule —rectal temperature on admission."

I thought to argue, or plead, or protest, but the expression on her face showed that this would be useless. Abjectly, I turned on my face, and the leg, unsupported, fell and prolapsed excruciatingly at the knee.

Nurse Solveig inserted the thermometer and disappeared—disappeared (I timed it) for more than twenty minutes. Nor did she answer my bell, or come back, until I set up a shindy.

"You should be ashamed of yourself!" she said, as she returned, her face pink with rage.

The patient next to me, a young man quite breathless from severe asbestosis, with a good colloquial knowledge of English, whispered, "She's a horror, that one. But the others are nice."

After my temperature had been taken, I was carted off to have the leg X-rayed.

All went smoothly until the technician, unthinkingly, lifted up the leg by the ankle. The knee buckled backwards and instantly dislocated, and I am afraid I let out an involuntary howl. Seeing what had happened, she immediately put a hand under the knee to support it, and very gently, tenderly, lowered it to the table.

"I am so sorry," she said. "I didn't realize at all."

"That's fine," I said. "No harm has been done. It was a complete accident. With Nurse Solveig it's deliberate."

I waited on the stretcher while the doctor was checking my X-rays. She was a local G.P., a nice motherly woman, who was covering the hospital that night for emergency call. No fractures of the long bones, she said—one couldn't really examine or X-ray the knee. She'd never seen such an injury before, but thought it was probably no more than a torn quad, though this could only be determined at surgery. It was quite a big operation, she said—"but straightforward," she added at once, with a smile, seeing my obvious fear. I might be laid up as much as three months. "Probably less, but you should be prepared." I would be wisest to get it done in London, she said. The Red Cross would arrange transport to Bergen—a pretty road if one was in the mood—and there were lots of planes from Bergen to London. . . .

I phoned my brother, a doctor in London. He sounded concerned, but I quickly reassured him. He told me he would arrange everything, and not to worry.

But worry one does, and as I lay there in my hospital bed at Odda—I had been returned to bed after seeing the doctor—with the breathless, coughing young man to one side and a poor old fellow, a *moribundus*, with an IV, on the other, I felt miserably anxious. I tried to sleep—they had given me a sedative—but it was difficult to get my mind off the leg, especially since the least movement of the knee caused sudden intense pain. I had to hold myself almost motionless, which did not conduce to sleep.

As soon as I began to drop off and, relaxing, moved involuntarily, I would be jerked awake by sudden violent pain in my knee. The good motherly doctor was consulted, and she advised that a temporary cast be put on, to immobilize the knee.

Back in bed, with my new cast, I fell instantly asleep, with my glasses on my face—for they were still there when I was woken at six from a dream that the entire leg was being squeezed in a vice. I woke to find that the leg was indeed being squeezed, though not by a vise. It had swollen up enormously—what I could see of it put me in mind of a vegetable marrow—and was obviously being constricted by the cast. The foot was very swollen, and cool from edema.

They incised the cast along its entire length on one side, and with the relief of pressure and pain I immediately fell asleep again, and slept soundly and well until a most amazing apparition entered the room, so that I rubbed my eyes thinking I was still dreaming. A young man—dressed, preposterously, in a white coat, for some reason—came in *dancing*, very lightly and nimbly, and then pranced round the room and stopped before me, flexing and extending each leg to its maximum like a ballet dancer. Suddenly, startlingly, he leapt on top of my bedside table, and gave me a teasing elfin smile. Then he jumped down again, took my hands and wordlessly pressed them against the front of his thighs. There, on either side, I felt a neat scar.

"Feel, yes?" he asked. "Me too. Both sides. Skiing . . . See!" And he made another Nijinski-like leap.

Of all the doctors I had even seen, or was later to see, the image of this young Norwegian surgeon remains most vividly and affectionately in my mind, because in *his own person* he stood for health, valor, humor—and a most wonderful, active empathy for patients. He didn't talk like a textbook. He scarcely talked at all—he acted. He leapt and danced and showed me his wounds, showing me at the same time his perfect recovery. His visit made me feel immeasurably better.

The ride to Bergen—six hours in the ambulance over mountain roads—was more than pretty. It was like a resurrection. Perched high on my stretcher, at the back of the ambulance, I feasted my eyes on the world I had so nearly lost. Never had it seemed so lovely, or so new.

Getting into the plane at Bergen was a nerve-racking experience. They weren't equipped to take a stretcher, so I had to be hoisted up the gangway and deposited obliquely across two first-class seats. I felt, for the first time, somehow peevish and fretful, with a sort of irritable-anxious restlessness which I was hard to put to control.

The captain, a big burly man, like an old buccaneer, was sensible and kind.

"No use fretting, son," he said, putting a huge hand on my shoulder. "First thing about being a patient—you have to learn patience!"

As I was taken in the ambulance from London airport, to the great hospital where I was to be operated the next day, my good humor and sanity began to leave me, and in their place came a most terrible dread. I cannot call it the dread of death, though doubtless that was contained in it. It was rather a dread of something dark and nameless and secret—a nightmarish feeling, uncanny and ominous, such as I had not experienced on the Mountain at all. Then, on the whole, I had faced what reality had in store, but now I felt distortion rising, taking over. I saw it, I felt it, and I felt powerless to combat it. It would not go away, and the most I could do was to sit tight and hold fast, murmuring a litany of reassurance and commonsense to myself. That journey in the ambulance was a bad trip, in all ways—and behind the dread (which I could not vanquish as its creator), I felt delirium rocking my mind—such a delirium as I used to know, all too well, as a child, whenever I was feverish or had one of my migraines. My brother, who was riding with me, observed some of this, and said:

"Easy now, Ollie, it won't be so bad. But you *do* look dead white, and clammy and ill. I think you've a fever, and you look toxic and shocked. Try and rest. Keep calm. Nothing terrible will happen."

Yes, indeed I had a fever. I felt myself burning and freezing. Obsessive fears gnawed at my mind. My perceptions were unstable. Things seemed to change—to lose their reality and become, in Rilke's phrase, "things made of fear." The hospital, a prosaic Victorian building, looked for a moment like the Tower of London. The wheeled stretcher I was placed on made me think of a tumbril, and the tiny room I was given, with its window blocked out (it had been improvised at the last minute, all the wards and side-wards being taken), put me in mind of the notorious torture chamber, "Little Ease," in the Tower. Later, I was to become very fond of my tiny womb-like room, and because it was windowless, I christened it "The Monad." But on that ghastly, ominous evening of the

25th, seized by fever and fantastical neurosis, shaking with secret dread, I perceived everything amiss and could do nothing about it.

"Execution tomorrow," said the clerk in Admissions.

I knew it must have been "*Operation* tomorrow," but the feeling of execution overwhelmed what he said. And if my room was "Little Ease," it was also the Condemned Cell. I could see in my mind, with hallucinatory vividness, the famous engraving of Fagin in his cell. My gallows-humor consoled me and undid me and got me through the other grotesqueries of admission. (It was only up on the ward that humanity broke in.) And to these grotesque fantasies were added the realities of admission, the systematic depersonalization which goes with becoming-a-patient. One's own clothes are replaced by an anonymous white nightgown, one's wrist is clasped by an identification bracelet with a number. One becomes subject to institutional rules and regulations. One is no longer a free agent; one no longer has rights; one is no longer in the world-at-large. It strictly analogous to becoming a prisoner, and humiliatingly reminiscent of one's first day at school. One is no longer a person—one is now an inmate. One understands that this is protective, but it is quite dreadful too. And I was seized, overwhelmed, by this dread, this elemental sense and dread of degradation, throughout the dragged-out formalities of admission, until —suddenly, wonderfully—humanity broke in, in the first lovely moment I was addressed as myself, and not merely as an "admission" or *thing*.

Suddenly into my condemned cell a nice jolly Staff-Nurse, with a Lancashire accent, burst in, a person, a woman, sympathetic—and comic. She was "tickled pink," as she put it, when she unpacked my rucksack and found fifty books and a virtual absence of clothes.

"Oh, Dr. Sacks, you're potty!" she said, and burst into jolly laughter.

And then I laughed too. And in that healthy laughter the tension broke and the devils disappeared.

As soon as I was settled in, I was visited by the Surgical Houseman and Registrar. There were some difficulties about "the history," because they wanted to know the "salient facts," and I wanted to tell them everything—the entire story. Besides, I wasn't quite certain what might or might not be "salient" in the circumstances.

They examined me as best they could with a cast. It seemed to be no more than an avulsed quadriceps tendon, they said, but complete examination would only be possible under general anesthesia.

"Why general?" I asked. "Couldn't it be done under spinal?"

For then I could *see* what was happening. They said, no, general anesthesia was the rule in such cases, and besides (they smiled) the surgeons wouldn't want me talking or asking questions all through the operation!

I wanted to pursue the point, but there was something in their tone and manner that made me desist. I felt curiously helpless, as with Nurse Solveig in Odda, and I thought: "Is *this* what "being a patient" means? Well, I have been a doctor for fifteen years. Now I will see what it means to be a patient."

I was exaggeratedly upset. As soon as I thought about it, I recognized it readily. They hadn't meant to sound inflexible or peremptory. They seemed pleasant enough, in an impersonal way: doubtless they lacked authority in the matter; I would do best to ask my surgeon in the morning. They had said that my operation was scheduled for 9:30, and that the surgeon—a Mr. Swan—would look in to see me first for a chat.

I thought, "Damn it, I hate the idea of being put under, and relinquishing consciousness and control." Besides, more important, my entire life had been directed towards awareness and observation—was I to be denied the opporutnity of observation *now*?

I phoned up my family and friends, to let them know what had happened, and was happening, and to say that if I should, by malchance, die on the table, I wished and willed them to make suitable extracts from my notebooks and other unpublished writings, and publish these as they thought fit.

After phoning them, I felt I should make it more formal, and so I wrote everything out in legal-sounding language, dated it, and asked two nurses to witness my signature. Feeling that I had "taken care" of everything— or everything it was in my power to take care of—I had no difficulty falling asleep; and I slept well and deeply until a little after five, when I woke with a foul dry mouth, feeling a bit feverish, and with a throbbing in my knee. I asked for some water, but was told "NPO"—nothing by mouth the day of operation.

I waited eagerly for Swan to come. Six o'clock, seven o'clock, eight o'clock. . . . Wasn't he coming, I asked Sister, a formidable-looking woman in severe dark blue (the jolly Staff-Nurse of the night before had been in a striped uniform).

"Mr. Swan will come when he pleases," she said tartly.

At 8:30 a nurse came in to give me my premeds. I said I needed to speak to the surgeon about spinals. No problem, she said: one got the same premeds for a general and a spinal.

I wanted to say that I might be muzzy from the premeds and unable to think clearly when Mr. Swan came. She said not to worry, he'd be here any moment, before the premeds had time to act. I let the matter rest—I took it.

Very soon I had a dry mouth, and phosphenes— spots and flashes in front of the eyes—and something of a dreamy-silly feeling. I rang for staff-nurse. It was 8:45— I hadn't taken my eyes off the watch since the injection— and asked what I had been given. The usual, she said —phenergan and hyoscine, such as they use for "twilight sleep." I groaned inwardly—I would be unmanned, softened up by medication.

Mr. Swan made his appearance at 8:53 and found me gazing at my watch. I had a momentary impression of a very shy man, but this was instantly effaced by his brisk, hearty voice.

"Well," he said loudly. "How are we doing today?"

"Bearing up," I replied, and my voice sounded muzzy.

"Nothing to worry about," he continued briskly. "You've torn a tendon. We reconnect it. Restore continuity. That's all there is to it . . . nothing at all!"

"But . . ." I said slowly—but he had already gone from the room.

With a great effort, because I felt dragged down and somehow lazy from the premeds, I rang the bell and asked for Sister.

"What is it?" she said. "Why have you called me?"

"Mr. Swan," I said enunciating my words carefully. "He didn't stay very long. He was just in and out. He seemed to be in an awful hurry."

"Well, I never," Sister huffed. "He's a very busy man. You're lucky he looked in at all."

A last memory—before going under. . . . The anesthetist had asked me to count aloud, while he injected Pentothal IV. I watched, curiously emotionless, as he entered the vein, drew up some blood to make sure and slowly injected. I noticed nothing—no reaction whatever. When I got to nine, some impulse made me glance at the clock. I wanted to catch my last moment of consciousness and, perhaps, by concentrating, hold on to it. As soon as I looked, I saw something was amiss.

"The second hand," I said, drunkenly clearly. "Has it actually stopped, or is it an illusion?"

The anesthetist glanced up, and said, "Yes, it's stopped. Must be stuck."

And with this I lost consciousness, for I remember no more.

My next memory, or first memory on coming round, does not quite deserve the word "next." I was lying in bed and had the impression that someone was shaking me or calling my name. I opened my eyes and found the House-man leaning over me.

"How do you feel?" he said.

"How do I feel?" I replied, in a voice so coarse and violent I scarcely recognized it as my own. "I'll tell you how I feel! I feel fucking awful! What the hell's going on? A few minutes ago my knee felt fine, and *now* it feels like hell—fucking hell!"

"That wasn't a few minutes ago, Dr. Sacks," he replied. "That was seven hours ago. You've had an operation, you know."

"Good God!" I said, stunned. It hadn't occurred to me that I had had, or might have had, an operation. There was no sense whatever of any "nextness" or "in-between"—that time had passed, or that anything had "happened."

"Well, well," I said, sobered. "How did it go?"

"Fine," he said blandly. "No problems at all."

"And the knee," I went on. "Was that thoroughly explored?"

He hesitated, or seemed to hesitate, a bit. "Don't worry," he said, finally. "The knee should be fine. We didn't go into it. We felt it was OK."

I wasn't entirely reasured by what he said, or by his tone when saying it, and my last thought, before sinking into the depths again, was that they might have overlooked some quite crucial injury to the knee, and that maybe I wasn't in quite trustworthy hands.

Apart from the conversation with the Houseman, which I remembered precisely, and have recorded practically verbatim, I have almost no coherent memories of the 48 hours following the operation. I was quite feverish, shocked, and toxic, and there was intense pain in my knee. I was given doses of morphine every three hours. I had periods of delirium, of which I remember nothing. I felt horribly sick and intensely thirsty, but was only allowed rare sips of water. I couldn't pass my urine, and had to have a catheter inserted. These two days were a lost two days.

I didn't really come to, then, till the Wednesday evening, two days after the operation—two days which were

pretty much lost, at least so far as any coherent and con-
secutive consciousness was concerned. I revived rather
suddenly, with the fever and delirium gone, and the pain
so much better that the injections could be stopped, and
the catheter—yes, the catheter, that abomination—was
taken out, and I could enjoy the pleasure of pissing freely.
I felt wonderfully refreshed in mind and body, which may
sound strange for someone who had had quite a major operation, was shocked from tissue destruction, and feverish
and delirious into the bargain, but this is the way. One
bounces back, as they say, re-invigorated, regenerated. One
is almost a new man.

A sharp sweet breeze was blowing through the win-
low—a sweet evening breeze, carrying with it the sounds
of birds at evensong in the quadrangle outside. I took a
deep breath with delight, and murmured a prayer of
thanksgiving at this speedy—and, yes, luscious—recovery.
Having thanked God, I thanked the surgeon and the staff
for pulling me through, and all the good folk in Norway
too who had brought me to safety. Ninety-six hours ago,
I reflected, I had been groping in the dusk on a chill mountain in Norway, in a land of darkness, and the shadow of
death. God be praised that I was back in the land of the
living!

I stretched luxuriously—and this action, as I pulled
on the plaster, suddenly reminded me that I had a cast—
and, yes, indeed, a leg in the cast! Well, there it was—a
little bit of it anyhow, a rim of thigh at the top, and my
foot, pink and lively, if rather swollen, at the bottom. It
was splendid to think that continuity was restored, the tendon reconnected, and everything in good order. All was
well, and all would be well. It would take time, no doubt.

I had to anticipate a month or so in hospital, and then a couple of months convalescence. There would be some wasting of muscle under the cast—I had often seen how quickly the quadriceps wasted with bedrest and disuse—and I could not expect an instant return of full strength and use to the leg. . . . All this I understood, and accepted—accepted gladly. It was a small price to pay for my delivery from death or devastating, permanent disability. The vital point, surely, was this: that I had, as by a miracle, survived my accident, that my injury had been repaired by an excellent surgeon, that a careful search at operation had found nothing damaged other than the tendon, that recovery should be straightforward, and that no "complications" of any sort had been encountered, or were to be expected.

It would be good to tense the quadriceps again, to *feel* again my power and control, which had been so disquietingly lost when the tendon was ruptured. Now it was united again, I would get the muscle going again, and build it up as fast as I could. I knew well how to build up muscle and strength, being an old hand at this from my weight-lifting days. I would amaze everybody, and show what I could do!

Smiling with anticipation, I tensed the quad—and, inexplicably, nothing happened, *nothing at all*. At any rate I didn't feel anything—but I hadn't been looking. Perhaps there had only been a small contraction. I tried again—a strong pull this time—watching the quadriceps closely at the top of the cast. Again nothing—no visible motion whatever, not the least trace of any contraction. The muscle lay motionless and inert, unmoved by my will. Tremblingly I put down my hand to feel it. It was tremendously wasted, for the cast (which had presumably been snug after surgery) now allowed me to put my entire fist underneath it.

Some atrophy, at least, was only to be expected, on the basis of disuse. What I did *not* expect, and what struck me as exceedingly strange and disquieting was to find the muscle completely limp—most horribly and unnaturally limp—in a way one would never find with disuse alone. Indeed, it scarcely felt like muscle at all—more like some soft inanimate jelly or cheese. It had none of the springiness, the tone, of normal muscle; and it wasn't just "flabby"—it was completely *atonic*.

I had a qualm of absolute horror, and shuddered; and then the emotion was immediately repressed or suppressed. I hurriedly shifted my attention to pleasanter things. This was very easy to do. Doubtless I'd find that I'd been making some absurd mistake—like putting the key upside-down in the lock—and discover that everything was working OK in the morning.

My father, and old friends, would be dropping in soon—I had asked Staff to spread the word that I was conscious, and "receiving." And as for that nonsense with the leg—well, it was just that, nonsense. The physiotherapist would be coming in the morning, and we'd put the damn thing through its paces.

I had a splendid evening—a celebration really. It was lovely to have my old friends about me, my friends whom I had "dreamt about" when, as I thought, I was dying on the Mountain. (I told them the story, but I didn't tell them *that*.) It was a lovely, happy, convivial evening in which, to the Night Supervisor's amusement and outrage, we split a magnum of champagne between us. It was deeply reassuring to my friends as well, for I had declined to see them on Sunday evening, but had phoned them up, frighteningly, asking that they be my executors, if something "happened." Well, nothing had happened—and I was exuberantly alive. I was alive, and they were alive. We were all alive, and contemporaries, and living together, travelling companions on the journey of life. That evening, the 28th, amid my friends' smiles and laughter (and sometimes tears), I felt, as never before, what conviviality meant—not just being alive, but sharing life, being alive *together*. I had felt my aloneness on the Mountain as being, in a sense, almost sadder than death.

It was such a good evening, so festive, that we were reluctant to break up.

"How long do you think you're going to be in this joint?"

"Not a minute longer than necessary—just as soon as I can walk out of it. I should be running around in a couple of weeks."

I lay in a glow of good feeling and good fellowship when they left, and then, in a few minutes, drifted off to sleep.

But all was *not* well, down in the depths. I had, indeed, had a momentary qualm about my leg, but I had managed—I thought successfully—to dismiss this as something "silly," some kind of "mistake," and it certainly cast no shadow on my spirits in our convivial evening. I had indeed "forgotten" it, forgotten all about it; but down in the depths it had not been forgotten.

And in the night, when I descended to the depths (or the depths erupted and surfaced in me) I had a dream of peculiar horror, which was the more horrific as it seemed so literal and undream-like. I was on the Mountain again,

impotently struggling to move my leg and stand up. But—
and this, at least, was a dream-like conflation—there was a
peculiar confusion of past and present. I had just had my
fall, and yet the leg was sewn up—I could *see* the row of
tiny neat stitches. "Splendid!" I thought. "Continuity is
restored. They came along with a helicopter and sewed
me up on the spot! I'm all re-connected, I'm ready to go!"
But the leg, for some reason, didn't budge in the least,
even though it was so neatly and nicely sewn up. There
wasn't a twitch, not so much as the stirring of a single
muscle fiber, when I tried to use the leg and get to my feet.
I put my hand down, and felt the muscle—it felt soft and
pulpy, without tone or life. "Heavens above!" I said in my
dream. "There's something the matter—quite dreadfully
the matter. The muscle's been *denervated*, somehow or
other. It's not just the tendon—the nerve-supply's gone!"
I strained and strained, but it was no use at all. The leg
lay motionless, and inert, as if dead.

I woke from this dream, sweating, in terror, actually
trying to tense the flaccid muscle (as, perhaps, I had been
doing in my dream). But it was useless, it didn't work—
as in the dream. I said to myself: "It's the champagne.
You're delirious, you're excited. Or perhaps you're not
awake, but in another dream. Go back to sleep—deep
restful sleep—and you'll find that everything's OK in the
morning."

I fell asleep, but entered dreamland once again. I was
on a riverbank overgrown with enormous lush trees, whose
shadows dappled the slightly rippling water. It was sublimely quiet, almost tangibly quiet, the deep quiet wrap-
ping me round like a mantle. I had my binoculars and
camera with me. I was out to sight an extraordinary new

fish—a wonderful thing, it was said, though few people had ever seen it. I understood that it was called a "Chimaera." I waited patiently, by its lair, for a while, and then whistled and clapped, and threw a stone in the water, to see if I could arouse the indolent beast.

Suddenly, very suddenly, I saw a motion in the water, a stirring which seemed to come from unimaginable depths. The waters appeared to be being sucked in at the middle, leaving a vast space, a vastation, a vast gurgitation. Myth had it that the Chimaera could swallow the whole river at one gulp, and in this moment my wonder changed to terror, because I realized that the myth was literally true. From the vast space of his creation, the Chimaera arose, rose up from the depths in majestic splendor, all milky-white, furrowed, like Moby Dick—except, unbelievable!—he had horns on his head, and the face of a vast browsing animal.

Now, outraged, he turned his gaze on me—with immense bulbous eyes, like the eyes of a bull, but a bull which could draw a whole river into his mouth, and with a vast scaly tail as big as a cedar.

As he turned—his vast face towards me, his vast eyes upon me—a wild and terrible panic overcame me, and frantically I tried to leap backwards up towards safety, *up* the river bank behind me. But I couldn't spring. The movement came out wrong and instead of throwing me backwards threw me violently forwards, beneath what I now saw were the *hooves* of the fish. . . .

The violence of my sudden movement jerked me awake, and I found that I had contracted my hamstrings most violently in my sleep, to the limit. My right heel had actually kicked my buttock, while my left heel was ground into the edge of the cast. It was a bright shining morning. This much I could see, for light could come in, to say nothing of wind, sounds, and scents (it was only vision, pattern, detail, which was blocked by the scaffolding rising outside barely a foot from the window). A bright Thursday morning—and I could hear the tea-trolley in the corridor, and smell buttered toast! I suddenly felt wonderful—this was the very morning of life: I sucked in the good air, and forgot my foul dreams.

"Tea or coffee, Dr. Sacks?" asked the little Javanese nurse. (I had seen her, and liked her, briefly noticing her on that dread morning of surgery.)

"Tea," I replied. "A whole pot of tea! And porridge, and poached eggs, and buttered toast with marmalade!"

She looked at me wide-eyed, almond-eyed, sweet-eyed, amazed. "Well, you *are* better today!" she said. "You wanted nothing but sips of water the last two days. I'm very glad for you now that you feel good again."

Yes, so was I. I felt good and glad, a returning vigor, and a desire for exercise and movement. I had always been active—activity was vital. I loved all motion, the quick motion of the body, and hated the thought of lying idle in bed.

I spotted a monkey-bar, a sort of trapeze, suspended from the bed. I reached up to it, grabbed tight, and did twenty chin-ups. Lovely movement, lovely muscles—their action gave me joy. I rested, and did another set—thirty this time—and then lay back savoring the good feeling.

Yes, I was still in good shape—injury, surgery, tissue-damage notwithstanding. That was damn good to do fitfy chin-ups, considering I'd been delirious, and in shock, only fifteen hours before. It gave me not only gladness, but confidence as well—confidence in my good body, its strength, its resilience, its will to recovery.

After breakfast, I had been told, the physiotherapist would be coming. She was absolutely first-class, everyone said, and we'd start work together—get that leg of mine toned up, ship-shape, and working with the rest. I somehow *felt* like a ship when I said "ship-shape" to myself, a living ship, a ship of life. I felt my body was the ship in which I travelled through life, all parts of it—strong timbers, alert sailors working harmoniously together, under the direction and co-ordination of the captain, myself.

A little after nine the physiotherapist came in, a powerful hockeyish woman with a Lancashire accent, accompanied by an assistant or student, a Korean girl with demure, downcast eyes.

"Dr. Sacks?" she roared, in a voice as might carry across an entire field.

"Madam!" I said quietly, inclining my head.

"Happy to meet you," she said, somewhat less loudly, giving me her hand.

"Happy to meet *you*," I replied, somewhat less softly, giving her mine.

"How's the old leg? How's it feeling? Probably hurts like Billy-O, what?"

"No, doesn't hurt much now—just an occasional flash. But it seems sort of funny—not working right."

"Mmm!" she harrumphed, considering for a moment. "Well, let's have a look, and get down to work."

She pulled back the sheet, revealing the leg, and as she did so I saw a sudden startled look on her face. It was instantly replaced by a serious, sober expression of professional concern. She seemed, all of a sudden, less bouncy, more subdued and methodical. Taking out a tape measure, she measured the thigh and then, for comparison, the good side. She seemed disbelieving of the measurements, and repeated them again, throwing a brief glance at the silent Korean.

"Yes, Dr. Sacks," she said at last. "You've quite a bit of wasting—the quadriceps down seven inches, you know."

"That sounds a lot," I said. "But I suppose it atrophies pretty quickly from disuse."

She seemed relieved at the sound of the word "disuse." "Yes, disuse," she muttered, less to me than herself. "I'm sure it can all be explained by disuse."

She put down her hand again, and palpated the muscle, and again I thought I saw a startled and disturbed look, and even a trace of unguarded disgust, as when one touches something which is unexpectedly soft and squirmy. Seeing this expression—which was, again, effaced in an instant, and replaced by a bland professional look—all my own fears, suppressed, came back redoubled.

"Well," she said—and again that over-loud, hockey-field voice. "Well," she bellowed, "enough of all this—feeling, measuring, talking, and what-not. Let's *do* something."

"What?" I asked, mildly.

"Contract the muscle—what do you think? I want you to tense the quad on this side—don't need to tell you how. Just tense the muscle. Firm it up now—firm it up right under my hand. Come on, you're not trying. Do it with this one."

Instantly and powerfully I tensed the quad on my right. But there was no trace of tensing, no firming up, when I tried on the left. I tried again—and again, and again—without result.

"I don't seem to be very good at this," I said in a small voice.

"Don't be discouraged," she roared. "There's lots of different ways. A lot of people find tensing—isometric contraction—tricky. One needs to think of a movement, not a muscle. After all, people move, they *do* things, they don't tense their muscles. Here's your patella—right under the cast." She rapped the cast with her strong fingers and it emitted an odd chalky, inorganic sound. "Well, just pull it towards you. Pull your knee-cap right up—you'll have no difficulty now the tendon's been fixed."

I pulled. Nothing happened. I pulled again, and again. I pulled till I was grunting and panting with exertion. Nothing happened, nothing whatever, not the least shiver or quiver of movement. The muscle lay motionless as a deflated balloon.

The physiotherapist was beginning to look flustered and frustrated, and said to me severely, in her games-mistress voice: "You're not trying, Sacks! You're not really trying!"

"I'm sorry," I said weakly, wiping the sweat off my brow. "It seems to me I was putting in a lot of effort."

"Well, yes," she said, grudgingly. "It looked like hard work—and yet nothing happened! Well, not to worry, we've got other ways! Pulling on the patella is still isometric in a way—and it may be more difficult because you can't *see* your patella." She rapped the opaque cast with her knuckles this time, as if knocking for admittance.

"It would be nice if they made transparent casts," I suggested.

She nodded vigorously. "And better still if they didn't use casts at all. They're great clumsy objects, and cause all sorts of problems. They'd do much better to immobilize joints with a brace—but you could never tell that to an orthopedist. A fat lot they know about physiotherapy!" She stopped suddenly, embarrassed. "I didn't mean to say that," she said, in a voice very far from her games-mistress one. "It just came out! But . . ." She hesitated, and then, finding understanding and encouragement in my face, went on: "I'm not saying anything against orthopods—they do a wonderful job—but they never seem to think of movement and posture—how you *do* things once the anatomy's been put right."

I thought of Swan's lightning visit just before surgery, and of his saying: "We reconnect it. Restore continuity. That's all there is to it." I found myself taking to this good physiotherapist.

"Miss Preston," I said, glancing at her name-tag (I had only thought of her as "the physiotherapist" up to this point). "I think you are talking very good sense indeed and I wish more doctors thought as you do. Most of them have got their heads in a cast"—and now it was my turn to rap the chalky cylinder for empasis—"but coming back to me, what shall I try now?"

"I'm sorry," she said. "I got carried away. . . . Let's have another go. It's all plain sailing once the muscle gets going. One little contraction—that's all you need—it's that first little twitch, and then you go from there. I'll tell you what—" here her voice became sympathetic and friendly—"I was just supposed to do isometrics with you today, but it's very important you have a success. I know how upsetting it is to keep trying—and fail. It's very bad to end up with a miserable sense of failure. We'll try *active* contraction—and something you can see. They don't want you lifting your leg, but I'll take all the weight. I'm going to lift your left leg nice and gently off the bed, and all you do is join in and help me. . . . We have to get you sitting up a bit." She nodded to the young Korean student, who bolstered up the pillows till I was in a sitting position. "Yes, that should bring in the hip-flexor action nicely. Ready?"

I nodded, feeling Yes, this woman understands, she'll help me get it going if anyone can, and prepared myself for an almighty effort.

"You don't have to brace yourself like that," laughed Miss Preston. "You're not trying for one of your weight-lifting records. All you do, now, is to lift up with me. . . . Up, up. . . . Do it with me. . . . Just a little bit more. . . . Yes, it's coming now . . ."

But it wasn't coming. It didn't come, nothing came at all. And I could see this in Miss Preston's face, as I saw it with the leg. It was a dead-weight in her hands—without any tone or motion or life of its own—like jelly, or pudding, packed in a cast. I saw my own concern and disappointment writ large, undisguised, on Miss Preston's face, which had lost its facade of professional indifference, and become alive and open, transparent and truthful.

"I *am* sorry," she said (and I knew she was sorry). "Perhaps you didn't quite get it that time. Let's try again."

We tried, and tried, and tried, and tried. And with each failure, each defeat, I felt more and more futile, and the chances of success seemed smaller and smaller, and the sense of impotence and futility grew stronger and stronger.

"I know how much you're trying," she said. "And yet, it's like you're not trying at all. You put out all this effort—but somehow the effort isn't managing to *do* things."

This was very much what I felt myself. I felt the effort diffuse uselessly, unfocussed, as it were. I felt that it had no proper point of application or reference. I felt that it wasn't really "trying," wasn't really "willing"—because all "willing" is willing *something*, and it was precisely that something which was missing. Miss Preston had said, at the start of our session, "Tense the quad. I don't need to tell you how." But it was precisely this "how," the very idea, which was missing. I couldn't think how to contract the quadriceps any more. I couldn't "think" how to pull the patella, and I couldn't "think" how to flex the hip. I had the feeling that something had happened, therefore, to my power of "thinking"—although only with regard to this one single muscle. Feeling that I had "forgotten" something—something quite obvious, absurdly obvious, only it had somehow slipped my mind. I tried with the right leg. No difficulty at all. Indeed I didn't *have* to "try" or "think." No effort of willing or thinking was needed. The leg did everything naturally and easily. I also tried—it was Miss Preston's last suggestion—"facilitation" she called it—to raise both legs simultaneously, in the hope that there might be some "overflow" or "transfer" from the good side. But, alas, not a trace! No "facilitation" whatever!

After forty minutes, then, which left both Miss Preston and me exhausted and frustrated, we desisted, and let the quad be. It was a relief to both of us when she went over the other muscles in the leg, having me move my foot and toes, and other movements at the hip—abduction, adduction, extension, etc. All of these worked spontaneously, instantly, and perfectly, in contradistinction to the quadriceps, which worked not at all.

The session with Miss Preston left me pensive, and grim. The strangeness of the whole thing, and the foreboding I felt—which I had managed to "forget" the previous day, though it returned in my dreams—now hit me with full force, and could no longer be denied. The word "lazy," which she had used, struck me as silly—a sort of catchword with no content, no clear meaning at all. There was something amiss, something deeply the matter, something with no precedent in my entire experience. The muscle was *paralyzed*—why call it "lazy"? The muscle was toneless—as if the flow of impulses in and out, such as normally and automatically maintain muscle tone, had been completely suspended. The neural traffic had stopped, so to speak, and the streets of the city were deserted and silent. Life—neural life—was suspended for the moment, if "suspended" was not itself too optimistic a word. The muscles relax during sleep, especially deep sleep, and the neutral traffic lessens, but never comes to a halt. The muscles keep going night and day, with a vital pulsation and circulation of minute impulses, which can be awakened, at any moment, into full activity.

Even in coma the muscles retain some activity. They are still ticking over at a very low rate. The muscles, like the heart, never stop during life. But my quadriceps *had* stopped, so far as I could judge. It was utterly toneless and paralyzed. It was *as if dead*, and not just "asleep"; and, being "dead," it could not be "awakened"—it would have to be—what word could I use?—*quickened*—to restore it to life. Awake and asleep: the quick and the dead.

It was the deadness of the muscle which so unnerved me. And deadness was something absolute, unlike
tiredness or sickness. This was what I had felt, and suppressed, the previous evening: the sense, the foreboding,
that the muscle was dead. It was, above all, its silence
which conveyed this impression—a silence utter and absolute, the silence of death. When I called to the muscle,
there was no answer. My call was not heard, the muscle
was deaf. But was this all? Would this suffice to give me
the impression of "silence"? When one calls, one hears
oneself calling—even if the call is not heeded, or falls on
deaf ears. Perhaps—and this thought made me shudder,
seeming to move me into another realm altogether, a realm
of infinitely more serious, even uncanny, possibilities—this
"silence" I spoke of, this sense of "nothing happening,"
did this not mean that in fact I had *not* called (or that if
I had called, I could not hear myself calling)? The
thought, or something like it—premonitory and precursory
—had been in the back of my mind, surely, in my session
with Miss Preston. This bizarre business of "trying," which
was not truly trying, this business of "willing," which was
not truly willing, this business of "thinking," which was
not truly thinking, this business of "recalling," which was
not truly recalling . . .

What was happening with me? I couldn't *try*, I
couldn't will, I couldn't think, I couldn't recall. I couldn't
think or recall how to make certain movements, and my
"efforts" to do so were delusory, derisory, because I had
lost the power to "call" to a part of myself, the power to
call *on* a part of myself. . . . It seemed to me now, as I
mused, more and more darkly, by myself, that the whole

business was much deeper, much stranger, than I could have conceived. I felt abysses opening beneath me. . . .

That the muscle was paralyzed, that the muscle was "deaf," that its vital impulsional pulsing flow, its "heart," had stopped—that it was, in a single word, "dead" . . . All of these things, disquieting in themselves, paled into insignificance compared with what was coming most appallingly into view to me now. For all these things, horrid as they might be, were entirely local and peripheral phenomena, and as such not affecting my essential being—*me*—any more than the loss of some leaves, or a branch, affect the deep life, the sap-flow, the roots, of a tree. But what was now becoming frightfully, even luridly, clear was that whatever had happened was not just local, peripheral, superficial—the terrible silence, the forgetting, the inability to call or recall—*this* was radical, central, fundamental. What seemed, at first, to be no more than a local, peripheral breakage and breakdown now showed itself in a different, and quite terrible, light—as a breakdown of memory, of thinking, of will—*not just a lesion in my muscle, but a lesion in me.* The image of myself as a living ship—the stout timbers, the good sailors, the directing captain, myself—which had come so vividly to my mind in the morning, now re-presented itself in the lineaments of horror. It was not just that some of the stout timbers were rotten and infirm, and that the good sailors were deaf, disobedient or missing, but that I, the captain, was no longer captain. I, the captain, was apparently brain-damaged—suffering from severe defects, devastations, of memory and thought. I fell very suddenly, and mercifully, into an almost swoon-like sleep.

My sleep, though profound, was suddenly, rudely

and bewilderingly broken by the little Javanese nurse, normally so sedate, who burst into my room and shook me awake. She had glanced through the transparent door-panel, before bringing me lunch, and what she saw had made her drop the tray and burst through the door.

"Dr. Sacks, Dr. Sacks," she cried, shrill with alarm. "Just look where your leg is—you'll have the whole thing on the floor!"

"Nonsense!" I said lazily. I was still half-asleep. "My leg is right here, in front of me, right where it should be."

"It isn't!" she said. "It's half off the bed. You must have moved in your sleep. Just look where you are!"

"Come on!" I said, smiling, not bothering to look. "A joke is a joke."

"Dr. Sacks, I am not joking! Please raise yourself, and look down and see."

Thinking she was still having me on—hospital wards are notorious for their practical jokes—I levered myself up. I had been flat on my back. I looked—and looked harder. The leg was not there! Incredibly, impossibly, the leg was not there!

Where *was* it? I spotted the cylinder of chalk way off to my left, sticking out at a funny angle to my trunk and indeed, as Nurse said, more than half off the bed. I must have kicked it here with my good leg, without knowing, while asleep. I had a sudden sense of utter confusion. I had felt the leg in front of me—or, at least, I had *assumed* it to be there (it had been there before, and I had received no information to the contrary)—but now I could see it wasn't there at all but had got shifted and rotated through almost ninety degrees. I had a sudden sense of mismatch, of profound incongruity—between what I imagined I felt and what I actually saw, between what I had "thought" and what I now found. I felt, for a dizzying, vertiginous moment, that I had been profoundly deceived, illuded, by my senses: an illusion—such an illusion—as I had never before known.

"Nurse," I said, and I found my voice trembling, "would you be so kind as to move the leg back? It's not too easy for me to shift it, lying flat like this."

"Of course, Dr. Sacks—and high time too! It's almost over the edge—and you did nothing but talk."

I waited for her to move it, but to my surprise she did nothing. Instead she bent over the bed, straightened up and started for the door.

"Nurse Sulu!" I yelled—and it was her turn to be startled. "What's going on? I'm still waiting, please, for you to move my leg back!"

She turned round, her almond-eyes wide with amazement.

"Now *you're* joking, Dr. Sacks! I *did* move your leg back."

For once, I was completely lost for words, and grabbing the monkey-bar I hauled myself into a sitting position. Indeed she wasn't joking—she *had* moved the leg back! She *had* moved it back, but I hadn't felt her do it. What the hell was going on?

"Nurse Sulu," I said, very sober and subdued, "I'm sorry I got excited. May I ask you a favor? Would you be kind enough, now I'm sitting up and can see, to take the cast by the ankle, and move it around—just move it, if you please, any way you want."

I watched her carefully, and narrowly, as she did so—lifting it up, lowering it, moving it to either side. I could see all these movements, but I couldn't feel them at all. I watched her intently as she took the leg and moved it—a little up, a little down, a little to either side.

"And now some really big movements, please, Nurse Sulu."

Gallantly—because it was heavy, dead-weight, and unwieldly, and floppy—she lifted it right up, in flexion, to a right angle, and then way out to the side, at a right angle again. I could see all the movements, but I couldn't feel them at all.

"Just one final short test, Nurse Sulu, if you don't mind." My voice (I observed, as from a distance) had assumed a quiet, matter-of-fact, "scientific" tone, concealing the abominable fear, the opening abyss, that I felt.

I closed my eyes, and asked her to move the leg once again—first small movements and, if I said nothing, huge movements, as before. Well, we would see! If you move a man's arm while he's looking, he might find it difficult to pick out the feel from the sight. They are so naturally associated that one is not used to distinguishing one from the other. But, if you ask him to close his eyes, he has no difficulty judging the tiniest passive movements—a fraction of a millimeter's excursion, with a finger, for example. And indeed it is this "muscle sense," as it was once called, before Sherrington investigated it and renamed it "proprioception"—it is this sense dependent on impulses from muscles, joints and tendons, usually overlooked because normally unconscious, it is this vital "sixth sense" by which the body knows itself, judges with perfect, automatic, instantaneous precision the position and motion of all its movable parts, their relation to one another, their alignment in space. There used to be another old word, still often used—*kinesthesia*, or the sense of movement—but "proprioception," less euphonious, seems an altogether better word, because it implies a sense of what is "proper"— that by which the body knows itself, and has itself as "property." One may be said to "own" or "possess" one's body—at least its limbs and movable parts—by virtue of a constant flow of incoming information, arising ceaselessly, throughout life, from the muscles, joints and tendons. One has oneself, one *is* oneself, because the body knows itself, confirms itself, at all times, by this sixth sense. I wondered how much the absurd dualism of philosophy since Descartes might have been avoided by a proper understanding of "proprioception." Perhaps indeed such an insight was hovering in the great mind of Leibniz, when he spoke of "minute perceptions" intermediating between body and soul, although . . .

"Dr. Sacks!" Nurse Sulu's voice broke in, sharp with impatience. "I thought you'd fallen asleep or something. My poor arms are aching, and you haven't made a sound. I've had a proper work-out with this great heavy cast of yours. I've moved it every way as far as it will go. Now don't tell me you didn't feel *that!*"

"Nurse Sulu," I said solemnly, "I felt nothing at all. In fact, I was still waiting for you to begin!"

Nurse Sulu shook her head, having helped me nobly, and took leave, shaking her head in bewilderment and incomprehension. "He seemed so nice, so normal, so sane, this morning," I imagined her thinking, behind her smooth Javanese brow, "and now he's acting weird!" She would have been far more disturbed had she seen my actions through the glass-panelled door; and still more disturbed had she had any conception of what I was thinking, experiencing, feeling. "Weird" she would have found much too feeble a word. Indeed she would have found no word in her language, my language, any language, to convey the inconceivable character of what I was experiencing.

As soon as she had taken her leave—I indicated that I had lost my appetite for lunch—I turned at once to my leg, with a keen, startled and almost fierce attention. And in that instant, I no longer knew it. In that instant, that very first encounter, *I knew not my leg*. It was utterly strange, not-mine, unfamiliar. I gazed upon it with absolute non-recognition. I have had—we all have had—sudden odd moments of non-recognition, *jamais vu*; they are uncanny while they last, but they pass very soon, and we are back in the known and familiar world. But this did not pass—it grew deeper and deeper—and stronger, and stranger.

The more I gazed at that cylinder of chalk, the more alien and incomprehensible it appeared to me. I could no longer feel it as "mine," as part of me. It seemed to bear no relation whatever to me. It was absolutely *not-me*—and yet, impossibly, it was attached to me—and even more impossibly, "continuous" with me.

It must be the cast, I said to myself. A great object like that—it would throw anyone off; although it was odd that only *now* should it disturb me so much. After all, I had been put in a cast at Odda on Saturday. Why should I now, the following Thursday, find it so strange—a ludicrous "object" with no relation to me. This wasn't how I had regarded it when it was put on at Odda—I had the clearest memory of finding it not only a protection and comfort, but somehow friendly and hospitable and warm, a nice cozy home which would lodge my poor leg till it was better. Now it didn't look "friendly," or "hospitable," or "warm" at all. Nor could I conceive how it had ever done so at any time in the past. On the other hand, it didn't seem "nasty," or "unfriendly," or "hostile"—it didn't seem anything: it had no qualities at all.

In particular, it no longer seemed a "home." I couldn't conceive it "housing" anything, let alone part of me. I had the feeling that it was either totally solid, or empty—but, in either case, that it contained nothing at all. I looked at the rim of toneless flesh above the cast, and then thrust a hand down inside. There was so much room, indeed, that I could put both hands in. The experience was inconceivably shocking and uncanny. The day before, when I had put my hand down and palpated the quadriceps, I had found it "horrible"—limp and pulpy, like a sort of soft, inanimate jelly or cheese. But the horror was nothing to what I felt now. The day before, touching it, I had at least touched *something*—unexpected, unnatural, unlifelike, perhaps—but nevertheless something; whereas today, impossibly, I touched nothing at all. The flesh beneath my fingers no longer seemed like flesh. It no longer seemed like material or matter. It no longer resembled anything. The more I gazed at it, and handled it, the less it was "there," the more it became Nothing—and Nowhere. Unalive, unreal, it was no part of me—no part of my body, or anything else. It didn't "go" anywhere. It had no place in the world.

> That which is not Body is no part of the Universe . . . and since the Universe is all, that which is not Body is Nothing—and No Where.
>
> —Hobbes

I had lost something—that was clear. I seemed to have lost "my leg"—which was absurd, for there it was, inside the case, safe and sound—a "fact." How could there be any doubt in the matter? And yet there was. On this very matter of "having" or "possessing" a leg, I was profoundly doubtful, fundamentally unsure.

When I closed my eyes, as a start, I had no feeling whatever of where the leg lay—no feeling that it was "here," as opposed to "there," no feeling that it was anywhere—no feeling at all. And what can be felt, what can be posited, about something that is "not there"? It seemed, indeed, as if it was this profound disturbance of proprioception, which had only been discovered and revealed by a fluke, though then investigated carefully by Nurse Sulu and myself—it seemed as if this, in particular, was somehow the "last straw." Serious problems and questions had already arisen, relating especially to the injured and operated muscle: its great atrophy, its atonia, its apparent paralysis. And questions of a "higher" sort, just before I fell asleep—the apparent breakdown in "know-how" and "idea," so that I could no longer "think" or "recall" how to make muscular movements involving the muscle. There was already something odd going on at this point. But a total, absolute, "existential" breakdown immediately followed, and seemed precipitated by, the discovery of the breakdown of sensation and feeling, for it was then, and only then, that the leg suddenly assumed an eerie character—or, more precisely, if less evocatively, lost all its character—and became a foreign, inconceivable *thing*, which I looked at, and touched, without any sense whatever of recognition or relation. It was only then that I gazed at it, and felt I don't know you, you're not part of

me, and, further, I don't know this "thing," it's not part
of anything. *I had lost my leg.* Again and again I came
back to these five words: words which expressed a central
truth for me, however preposterous they might sound to
anyone else. In some sense, then, I had lost my leg. It had
vanished; it had gone; it had been cut off at the top. I was
now an amputee. And yet not an ordinary amputee. For
the leg, objectively, externally, was still there; it had disappeared subjectively, internally. I was therefore, so to speak,
an "internal" amputee. Neurologically, neuropsychologi-
cally, this was the salient fact. I had lost the inner image,
or representation, of the leg. There was a disturbance, an
obliteration, of its representation in the brain—of this part
of the "body-image," as neurologists say. Part of the "inner
photograph" of me was missing. I could also use some of
the terms of ego-psychology, which had a more-than-
coincidental correspondence to those of neurology. I could
say that I had lost the leg as an "internal object," as a symbolic and affective "imago." It seemed, indeed, that I
needed both sets of terms, for the inner loss involved was
both "photographic" and "existential." Thus, on the one
hand, there was a severe perceptual deficit, so that I had
lost all feeling of the leg. On the other, there was a "sympathetic" deficit, so that I had lost much of my feeling *for*
the leg. Both were implied in the terms I used—the sense
of my personal, living, beloved reality having been replaced by a lifeless, inorganic, alien dissolution of reality.

What could cause such a profound, such a calamitous,
change, such a total breakdown of feeling-of and feeling-
for, such a total breakdown of neural image—and *imago*?
A long-forgotten memory came to me dating from the
time when I was a student or "clerk" on the neurology

wards. One of the nurses called me in considerable perplexity, and gave me this singular story on the phone: that they had a new patient—a young man—just admitted that morning. He had seemed very nice, very "normal," all day —indeed, until a few minutes before, when he awoke from a snooze. He then seemed excited and strange—"not himself" in the least. He had somehow contrived to fall out of bed, and was now sitting on the floor, "carrying on" and vociferating, and refusing to go back to bed. Could I come, please, and sort out what was happening?

When I arrived I found the patient lying on the floor by his bed and staring at one leg. His expression contained anger, alarm, bewilderment and amusement— bewilderment most of all, with a hint of consternation. I asked him if he would go back to bed, or if he needed help, but he seemed upset by these suggestions and shook his head. I squatted down beside him, and took the history on the floor. He had come in, that morning, for some tests, he said. He had no complaints, but the neurologists, feeling that he had a "lazy" left leg—that was the very word they had used—thought he should come in. He had felt fine all day, and fallen asleep towards evening. When he woke up he felt fine too, until he moved in the bed. Then he found, as he put it, "someone's leg" in the bed—*a severed human leg*, a horrible thing! He was stunned, at first, with amazement and disgust—he had never experienced, never imagined, such an incredible thing. He felt the leg gingerly. It seemed perfectly formed, but "peculiar" and cold. At this point he had a brainwave. He now "realized" what had happened: *it was all a joke!* A rather monstrous and improper, but a very original, joke! It was New Year's

Eve, and everyone was celebrating. Half the staff were drunk; quips and crackers were flying; a carnival scene. Obviously one of the nurses with a macabre sense of humor had stolen into the Dissecting Room and nabbed a leg, and then slipped it under his bedclothes as a joke while he was still fast asleep. He was much relieved at the explanation; but feeling that a joke was a joke, and that this one was a bit much, he threw the damn thing out of the bed. But—and at this point his conversational manner deserted him, and he suddenly trembled and became ashen-pale—*when he threw it out of bed, he somehow came after it—and now it was attached to him.*

"Look at it!" he cried, with revulsion on his face. "Have you ever seen such a creepy, horrible thing? I thought a cadaver was just dead. But this is uncanny! And somehow—it's ghastly—it seems stuck to me!" He seized it with both hands, with extraordinary violence, and tried to tear it off his body, and failing, punched it in an access of rage.

"Easy!" I said. "Be calm! Take it easy! I wouldn't punch that leg like that."

"And why not?" he asked, irritably, belligerently.

"Because it's *your* leg," I answered. "Don't you know your own leg?"

He gazed at me with a look compounded of stupefaction, incredulity, terror and amusement, not unmixed with a jocular sort of suspicion. "Ah Doc!" he said. "You're fooling me! You're in cahoots with that nurse—you shouldn't kid patients like this!"

"I'm not kidding," I said. "That's your own leg."

He saw from my face that I was perfectly serious—

and a look of utter terror came over him. "You say it's my leg, Doc? Wouldn't you say that a man should know his own leg?"

"Absolutely," I answered. "He *should* know his own leg. I can't imagine him *not* knowing his own leg. Maybe *you're* the one who's been kidding all along?"

"I swear to God, cross my heart, I haven't. . . . A man *should* know his own body, what's his and what's not—but this leg, this *thing*"—another shudder of distaste—"doesn't feel right, doesn't feel real—and it doesn't *look* part of me."

"What *does* it look like?" I asked in bewilderment, being, by this time, as bewildered as he was.

"What does it look like?" He repeated my words slowly. "I'll tell you what it looks like. *It looks like nothing on earth.* How can a thing like that belong to me? I don't know *where* a thing like that belongs. . . ." His voice tailed off. He looked terrified and shocked.

"Listen," I said. "I don't think you're well. Please allow us to return you to bed. But I want to ask you one final question? If this—this thing—is *not* your left leg" (he had called it a "counterfeit" at one point in our talk, and expressed his amazement that someone had gone to such lengths to "manufacture" a "facsimile") "then where *is* your own left leg?"

Once more he became pale—so pale that I thought he was going to faint. "I don't know, he said. "I have no idea. It's disappeared. It's gone. It's nowhere to be found. . . ."

I was deeply perturbed by the entire business—so deeply, indeed, I now reflected, that I had forgotten it for more than fifteen years, and although I called myself a neurologist I had totally forgotten him, thrust him out of my consciousness, until—until I found myself, apparently, in his position, experiencing (I could scarcely doubt it) what *he* had experienced, and, like him, scared and confounded to the roots of my being. It was clear that in some sense my symptoms were identical with this young man's—that they all went together to constitute an identical "syndrome."

Such a syndrome was first described in the last century by Anton and is occasionally referred to as "Anton's Syndrome," though he only picked out a few of its features. More had been delineated by the great French neurologist Babinski, who had coined the term "anosagnosia" for the singular unawareness that characterized such patients. Babinski had given memorable descriptions of the bizarre, almost comic, presentation in some cases: patients in whom the first sign of a stroke was an inability to recognize one side of their body—and the feeling that it was someone else's, or a "model," or a joke, so that they might turn to someone sitting next to them on a train, saying of their own hand, "Pardon me, Monsieur, you have your hand on my knee!" or, to a nurse clearing away the breakfast, "Oh, and that arm there—take it away with the tray!" And I thought of singular examples I had encountered myself: for instance, the patient at Mount Carmel who "discovered" his long-lost brother in his bed. "He's still attached to me!" he said indignantly. "The cheek of it! Here's his arm!" holding up, with his right hand, his own left arm. Babinski pointed out further that many such patients had been regarded as mad. Indeed they had a special category of madness tailor-made for them—*somatophrenia phantastica*, in Kraepelin's terminology. But this "madness" was extraordinarily specific and constant in its features, and not only occurred, often suddenly, in well-balanced people, who had shown no hints of any madness before, but was specifically associated with lesions of the brain—in particular of the posterior portions of the right hemisphere, which controlled the general awareness, or *gnosis*, of the left side of the body. Pötzl of Vienna had enriched these descriptions and had perhaps discussed their nature with Freud, comparing and contrasting them with somatic delusions. For Freud, who had been a neurologist, and a great one, in his youth (indeed he had coined the word *agnosia* in 1891) and who retained his neurological interests to the end, these delineations of Pötzl's syndrome (*optic-kinesthetic allesthesia*) would have been of quite extraordinary interest, as also to his daughter Anna, already eminent for her early studies in ego-psychology. What would have fascinated the Freuds, father and daughter, was that here was a specific pathophysiological syndrome, associated with damage in the posterior right hemisphere, which could produce specific and singular changes in body-identity—so that a patient might find a limb unfamiliar, or be unable to ascribe or relate it to himself, and (by way of rationalization and defense) might attribute it, if only temporarily, to someone else. There were also, Pötzl brought out, peculiar and specific changes in *affect*—as indeed was apparent in the preposterous (and often comic) aspect of the histories—when patients might nonchalantly wave a limb away, asking the nurse to be so kind as to remove it with the breakfast. Such patients, who showed perfectly normal reactions and affects in all other ways, might show an extraordinary indifference to the affected limbs. This, as Babinski noted, was one of the reasons why many of them had been diagnosed as having hysteria, schizophrenia or some other "dissociative" disorder. There *was*, indeed, a most striking "dissociation"— not only neurally, but emotionally and "existentially" too. This, however, was due not to "repression" of a concept and affect, but to a consequence of neural disconnection.

Very early in life, at Charcot's suggestion, Freud wrote a classic paper on the distinction of organic and hysterical paralyses, and he would have been deeply intrigued to find, towards the end of his life—Pötzl's syndrome was described in 1937—that *some* features which could easily have been taken as "hysterical"—the characteristic dissociation and bland or joking indifference— were, in those instances, entirely organic. More precisely, he would have been intrigued to find how a person and his ego-structure—which defined the boundaries of what was "me" and "not-me"—responded when faced with a massive body-agnosia. Had not Freud, himself rooted in physiology and biology, always said "The Ego is first and foremost a body Ego"?

Well, what now? Did *I* have Pötzl's syndrome? My case certainly looked indistinguishable from it! I could have been used as a classroom demonstration of this rare and singular "neuro-existential" pathology—and, for a moment, I imagined myself, Professor Dr. Anton-Babinski-Pötzl-Sacks, demonstrating a fascinating case of this syndrome—on myself! Then, as on the Mountain, I suddenly realized that this "fascinating case" *was* myself—not just a "case" for Dr. Anton-Babinski-Pötzl-Sacks to demonstrate and write up, but a very frightened patient, with a leg not only injured and operated upon but doubly disabled, indeed rendered useless, because it was no longer a part of my "inner image" of myself—having been erased from my body-image, and also my ego, by some pathology of the most serious and inexplicable kind.

With my poor patient, whom I had seen on that memorable New Year's Eve, emergency neurosurgery had disclosed a large vascular tumor overlying the right parietal lobe of the brain. It had actually started to bleed while he slept, so that by the time he awoke the "leg area"—that part of the brain in which the position and presence of the leg are represented—had been virtually obliterated. As a result it was impossible for him to feel his leg normally—to feel it as "present" or "part of himself," so that when he did discover it, it seemed to be a strange object introduced into his bed—"someone else's leg," "a corpse's leg," and, finally, a sort of uncanny, immaterial "counterfeit" leg. . . .

What, then, of myself? It was clear that I too had Pötzl's syndrome, with extinction of the left leg—and that I too, like my patient, must have some massive pathology in the right parietal lobe. "Physiology, anatomy, etiology" we are taught, and my mind, smooth and skilled, ran swiftly on these tracks. The physiology was that of right-hemisphere dysfunction; the anatomy, in correspondence, was a large "lesion" in this area. And the etiology, the cause, what was it? I could not doubt it for a moment: I had thrown an embolus, or dropped my blood-pressure, under anesthesia, and sustained in consequence a cerebral infarction, a massive "stroke" in my posterior right-hemisphere. "Anesthetic complication," they would write in the notes. . . .

To think it had come to this—that I had escaped, through a miracle, death or disastrous disability on the Mountain, that I had been brought, with infinite trouble, to one of the best orthopedic units in the world, only to succumb to a post-operative stroke! I visualized, in a single sweeping panorama, replete with the most minute and mortifying details, the wretched half-life which lay ahead of me with so massive a stroke—confined to a wheelchair, humilitatingly dependent, and with a leg at once so useless and "alien," so amputated internally, that it would be best and simplest to amputate it externally as well, which would at least relieve me of having to drag around a totally useless, functionless and indeed "defunct" limb. It ought to be removed as one would remove a mortified leg, because it *was*, in effect, mortified: it was neurally, functionally and existenially dead.

I lay engrossed in this vision, for an unconscionable time, in a sort of icy, fatalistic despair; groaning, meditating suicide and twiddling my toes. *My toes*! I had forgotten —*my toes were all right*! There they were, pink and lively, twiddling away, as if twiddling in mirth at my absurd train of thought! Grim and gloomy hypochondriac though I might have been, I was not ignorant of elementary neuroanatomy. A stroke massive enough to have knocked out the rest of the leg would certainly have knocked out the foot as well. As soon as this occurred to me, I burst into a hearty roar of laughter. My brain was all right—I hadn't had a stroke. I didn't know what I did have, but I didn't have a stroke.

I rang the bell and Nurse Sulu reappeared, concern writ large on her young placid face.

"What is it, Dr. Sacks? Are you all right?"

"Fine," I said. "Splendid. Never better! I find I have regained my appetite again. Do you think it would be possible to get me a sandwich or something?"

"My gracious goodness!" she said. "How you *do* change! When I left you looked terrible—pale, shivering, a dreadful look on your face. And now you seem fine! As you did back at breakfast."

"Well, I've been thinking a bit. I let myself get upset. . . . If a sandwich is difficult, just a cup of tea and a biscuit."

"But, Dr. Sacks, you can have your whole lunch. They're still serving it, you know."

"They are? How long is it since you were testing the leg out with me?"

She glanced at her watch. "Not ten minutes," she said. "Does it seem longer?"

Not ten minutes! I could hardly believe my ears. In that ten minutes, it seemed to me, I had been through a lifetime's experience. I had voyaged round a whole universe of thought. I had travelled so far—and they were still serving lunch!

Nurse Sulu brought me in a tray. I found myself quite ravenously hungry, which seemed very natural, after my physical and metaphysical exertions of the morning—hungry, and sensuous, craving the good things of the world.

My mind regurgitated, while eating, the words of the young man with the brain tumor who had "lost" his left leg. Fortunately for him, the tumor was benign, and prompt surgical intervention restored complete cerebral function. Perhaps he is alive now, and reading these words! I went to visit him, when he was convalescing, several weeks later, to see how he was doing, and whether he had any memories, or feelings, about his New Year's Eve.

The experience, he told me, was the most uncanny

and frightening in his life, and he wouldn't have believed it possible unless he had experienced it. He said—he repeated the word—it was "potty," it made no sense. One of his major fears was that he had gone completely mad. This was aggravated by his attempts to speak to the Staff, who kept telling him it was "nothing" and not to be "silly." He was very glad, very grateful, that I at least had listened —because even though I was a student, and "didn't know anything," I had tried to understand. He said he was glad, in a way, when the neurosurgeons (whom I had called in) assured him that it was "real," and not "in his mind"— even though he was very scared to think that he had a brain-tumor needing surgery. But even though the mechanism of the "extinction" was explained, along with the probability that his leg would "come back" when the pressure was removed, he found he couldn't believe it. It wasn't, he tried to explain, like an ordinary loss—when you misplace something somewhere. What was so awful about this sort of loss was that the leg hadn't been "misplaced," but had in fact lost its place. And since there was no longer any place it could come back to, he just didn't see how his leg *could* come back. This being so, nothing anyone said could really reassure him, and when they said his leg would "come back," he just nodded and smiled.

Yes, this was my position—my position exactly. The leg had vanished, taking its "place" with it. Thus there seemed no possibility of recovering it—and this irrespective of the pathology involved. Could memory help, where looking forward could not? No! The leg had vanished, taking its "past" away with it! I could no longer remember having a leg. I could no longer remember how I had ever walked and climbed. I felt inconceivably cut off from the person who had walked and run, and climbed just five days before. There was only a "formal" continuity between us. There was a gap—an absolute gap—between then and now; and in that gap, into the void, the former "I" had vanished—the "I" who could thoughtlessly stand, run and walk, who was totally and thoughtlessly sure of his body, who couldn't conceive how doubts about it could possibly arise. . . . Into that gap, that void, outside space and time, the reality and possibilities of the leg had passed, and disappeared. I had often thought the phrase "vanished into the blue" at once absurd, yet mysteriously significant. As if to rebuke my unbelief, my own leg had vanished "into the blue"; and, like the young patient with the bleeding brain-tumor, I couldn't imagine it returning in any "normal" or physical way, because it had vanished from space and time—vanished taking its space-and-time with it. If it went into the gap, the void, the "blue," it would have to come out of the gap, the void, the "blue": the eerie, stunning mystery of its going could only be matched by an equal mystery of coming or becoming. It had passed out of existence (whatever one meant by "existence"); and, by the same token, it would somehow have to come back *into* existence. My mind was dizzied with these thoughts of dissolution and recreation. The waters became deeper and deeper all the time; I dared not think too much, in case they closed over me.

As if to dissipate this metaphysical fog, there suddenly appeared, in my mind's eye, the robust and rumbustious figure of Dr. Johnson. My unconscious had summoned him to wake me from a Berkeleyan nightmare. I saw him with extraordinary clarity—and immediately loved him, and his strong commonsense. When asked his opinion of "the Berkeleyan doctrine"—the supposed un-reality of material objects—his reply had been to aim a mighty kick at a stone, saying "Bah! *Thus* I refute it!" I had always regarded this answer as quite perfect—theo-retically, practically, dramatically, comically: it was the obvious, the only thing to do—but it required Johnsonian genius to do it. For the answer to such questions is given by *acts*.

I had a vivid mental picture of Johnson kicking the stone—so vivid, so droll, I kept laughing to myself. But how could I apply Johnson's "test" to myself? I longed to aim at a mighty kick at a stone, and in so doing show the actuality of the kicking leg and the stone. But how could I kick with my unimaginable, "immaterial" leg? I could not make any contact with the stone. Thus the Johnsonian "test" would backfire on me, and its failure, or "untry-ability," would serve only to confirm the unreality of the leg, and sink it further into a Berkeleyan circle. The image of my stout and doughty champion faded. Even good Sam Johnson, if caught in my position, would be un-able to refute it.

Johnson's place, in my proscenium, was now taken by Wittgenstein—I fancied that the two men, seemingly so different, might get on rather well (I continually invent imaginary meetings and dialogues). I heard, in Wittgen-stein's voice, the opening words of his last work, *On Cer-tainty*: "If you can say, *Here is one leg*, we'll grant you all the rest. . . . The question is, whether it can make sense to doubt it." (And only later did I realize that my memory, or imagination, had interposed "leg" for "hand.") "Cer-tainty," for Wittgenstein, was grounded in the certainty of the body. But the certainty of the body was grounded in action. The answer to Wittgenstein's question as to whether one can be sure of one's hand, was to raise it, or sock someone in the face—as Samuel Johnson's answer was to kick the stone.

Johnson and Wittgenstein were in perfect agreement: one existed, and could show it, because one acted—because one could lift, or kick, a stone. I suddenly thought: a man with a phantom—a phantom leg—could not kick a stone.

I became all of a sudden desolate and deserted, and felt—for the first time, perhaps, since I had entered the hospital—the essential aloneness of the patient, a sort of solitude which I hadn't felt on the Mountain. Desperately now, I wanted communication, and reassurance, like the young patient who had brought out, though with difficulty and embarrassment, the sort of thing which had happened to him. I myself needed to communicate above all to my physician and surgeon: I needed to tell *him* what had happened to me, so that he could say, "Yes, of course, I understand."

I fell asleep and was woken by the arrival of my very favorite Aunt. I had half hoped she might come, but doubted if she would, because it was her birthday. Undaunted, at eighty-two, after a breakfast and a lunch with friends—and more, she said, would be coming for dinner —she had crossed London to have her birthday-tea with me, since I could not, as I usually did, go to have it with her. Suddenly remembering, at breakfast-time, that it was her birthday, I had prevailed upon Nurse Sulu, when she brought me breakfast, to procure a birthday-book for her, selecting, after some hesitation, *The Maiden Aunt in Fact and Fiction*. I gave this to her somewhat fearfully, saying

I hadn't read it, and maybe it was awful (though it was said to be excellent), and maybe she didn't like the category of "maiden aunt."

"But I *love* it!," she exclaimed, taking the book. "I love being a maiden aunt. I wouldn't be anything else. Especially a maiden aunt with eighty-seven nephews and nieces, two-hundred-and-thirty grand-nephews and nieces, and all the children I have taught—my children—for sixty years! So long as the book doesn't portray us as barren or lonely!"

"If it does," I said, "I'll send it back to the author!"

She rummaged in her bag and brought out a parcel. "And I've got a birthday-book for you. You were away on your birthday, up in the Arctic. I know you love Conrad. Have you read *this*?"

I unwrapped the parcel and found *The Rover*. "No, I haven't," I said, "but I like the title."

"Yes," she said. "It suits you. You've always been a rover. There are rovers, and there are settlers, but you're definitely a rover. You seem to have one strange adventure after another. I wonder if you will ever find your destination."

Over a lovely and tranquil tea—my good aunt had somehow persuaded the usually forbidding Sister to provide cress sandwiches and a huge pot of tea—under the affectionate and truthful gaze of my aunt, I related some of my discoveries that day.

She listened intently, not saying a word. "Dearest Bol," she said, when I drew my tale to a close, "you've been in some very deep waters, but these are the deepest." A shadow seemed to pass over her face. "Very deep waters," she murmured, half to herself. "Very deep and strange and dark. I wonder . . ." But I never learned what it was she wondered at the moment, because she emerged from her abstraction, broke off, looked straight at me, and said: "I can't begin to understand, but I am sure that it *can* be understood, and that after roving to-and-fro you will reach an understanding. You're going to have to be very clear and strong and bold. You're also going to have to bow your head, and be humble, and acknowledge that there are many things which pass the understanding. You mustn't be arrogant—and you mustn't be abject. And you mustn't expect too much from the surgeon. I'm sure he's a good man, and a first-rate surgeon, but this goes far beyond the province of surgery. You mustn't get angry if he doesn't understand completely. You mustn't expect the impossible of him. You must expect, and respect, limits. He'll have all sorts of limits—we all do. Professional limits, mental limits and emotional limits, most especially. . . . She stopped, arrested by some recollection or reflection. "Surgeons are in a peculiar position," she said, at last. "They face special conflicts. Your mother—." She hesitated, scanning my face. "Your mother was a dedicated surgeon, and a very gentle sensitive soul, and it was sometimes difficult for her to reconcile her human feelings with her surgery. Her patients were very dear to her, but as a surgeon she had to see them as anatomical and surgical problems. Sometimes, when she was younger, she seemed almost ruthless, but this was because her feelings were intense: she would have been overwhelmed by them, if she hadn't maintained a rigorous distance. It was only later that she achieved a balance—that essential balance of the technical and the personal."

"Be gentle, Bol!" she admonished me. "Don't *react*

to Mr. Swan. Don't call him "the Surgeon." It doesn't sound human! Remember he's human—as human as you are. All too human, probably, and even shyer than you are. All the trouble starts when people forget they're human."

Good, wise, simple words! If only I had heeded them! If only I had had that rare mildness and magnanimity which characterized my good aunt, that inner serenity and security which allowed her to face everything with a sweet and even humor, and never to exaggerate, distort or dismiss.

Over a second pot of tea—my aunt drank as much tea as Dr. Johnson!—the conversation became looser, slighter, easier, and the somber shadows, the terrible seriousness, which I had felt earlier, unable to withstand the playful atmosphere, seemed to dissolve and depart in the gay air.

As she gathered herself to leave, very suddenly, and in rapid succession, my aunt told me three jokes, of an astounding obscenity but delivered with a demure precision and propriety of utterance.

I burst out laughing with such violence, that I feared I would burst the stitches, and while I was laughing my aunt rose and left.

Yes, yes! Everything would be understood, set to rights, taken care of. All was well, and all would be well! There had been a minor complication, attributable to surgery, trauma, or both. The nature of this was a little hazy to me, but all would be made clear by Swan in the morning. He was a good man, I understood; he had had years of orthopedic experience; he must have seen this sort of thing hundreds of times before; I could count on a simple, reassuring diagnosis and prognosis. He would say—well, I didn't quite know what he would say, but he would say the right thing, and all would be well. Yes! I could confidently put myself in his hands—I should have thought of this before, instead of consuming myself in intense, solitary effort and thought. Thinking to help myself, I had quite needlessly over-alarmed myself.

What sort of a man would Swan be? I knew he was a good surgeon, but it was not the surgeon but the person I would stand in relation to, or, rather, the man in whom, I hoped, the surgeon and the person would be wholly fused. My encounter with the young surgeon in Odda had been perfect in its way. He was perfect for then, for that moment; but now my situation was more complex and obscure, and a heavier burden would rest on Mr. Swan. He could not flit in, dance, smile, and be gone; he had a heavy responsibility, the weight of caring for me for perhaps weeks or months. I ought not to demand too much of him, or over-burden him with the intensity of my distress. If he was a sensitive man he would be instantly aware of the distress and dispel it, with the quiet voice of authority. What I could not do for myself in a hundred years, precisely because I was entangled in my own patienthood and could not stand outside it, what seemed to me insuperably difficult, *he* could cut across at a single stroke, with the scalpel of detachment, insight and authority. He did not have to explain; he had only to act. I did not require an actuarial statement, such as "We see this syndrome in 60 per cent of all cases. It has been variously attributed to *x, y,* and *z.* The recovery rate is variously estimated as such-and-such, depending on this-and-that, and other imponderables." I required only the voice, the simplicity, the conviction, of authority: "Yes, I understand. It happens. Don't fret. Do this! Believe me! You will soon be well." Or words to that effect—words utterly direct and transparent, words without a hint of prevarication or indirection.

If he could not, in truth, reassure me with such words, I would want an honest acknowledgment of the fact. I would equally respect his integrity and authority if he said: "Sacks, it's the damndest thing—I don't know what you've got. But we'll do our best to find out." If he showed fear—frank fear—I should respect that too. I should respect whatever he said so long as it was frank and showed respect for me, for my dignity as a man. If he was frank and manly, I could take almost anything.

In the thought of Swan's visit, his understanding, his reassurance, I was permitted, at last, a profound repose. I had had the most bizarre and alarming day of my life— more bizarre and alarming, in its way, than my day on the Mountain. For there my fears, though ultimate, were natural and real—I could and I did confront the thought of death. But what now confronted me was *un*-natural and *un*-real. There was perplexity here of a terrible kind. . . . But Swan would understand this, he would have encountered it before: I could depend on him to say the right thing. How often had I myself, as a physician, mysteriously stilled the apprehensions of my patients—not through knowledge, or skill, or expertise, but simply by listening. I could not give myself repose, I could not be physician to myself; but another could. Swan would, tomorrow. . . .

Thus the day ended in a profound trusting sleep, a deep and dreamless sleep—at least for half the night. But then I fell into a succession of dreams, dreams of a most grotesque and uncanny sort, dreams of a kind I had never had before, neither in anxiety, in fever, in delirium, ever. . . . For hours, increasingly, I was the victim of these dreams. I would wake from them briefly, in startled horror, only to re-enter them the moment I slept again. In a sense they were scarcely like dreams at all—they had a monotony, a fixity, which was thoroughly undream-like—more like the repetition of some changeless physiological reality. For all I dreamed of was the leg—the non-leg. I repeatedly dreamt that the cast was solid, that I had a leg of chalk or plaster or marble, inorganic. I would be sitting in a chair, at dinner perhaps, or sitting on a park bench, enjoying the sun—these parts of the dream were simple and prosaic; but whatever I was doing—it was never standing or walking—there was that white stony cylinder in place of my leg, as fixed and motionless as that of a statue. Sometimes it was not plaster or marble, but something friable and incoherent, like sand or cement—and these dreams contained an additional fear—that there was nothing to hold the gritty mass together, no inner structure or cohesion, but a mere outer surface, visuality without substance. Frequently I dreamt that the cast-leg was perfectly hollow—though this is not quite an adequate word: not so much hollow as absolutely empty, a chalky envelope, a mere shell, about nothingness, a void. Sometimes it was a leg made out of mist, which retained, nevertheless, its motionless fixed shape; and sometimes—this was the worst—a leg made of darkness or shadow . . . or a leg impossibly made of nothing whatever. There was no change whatever in the dreams of that night. Or, rather, there were changes which were merely peripheral and incidental, in minor matters of setting and scene. At the center of each was this immovable, immaterial, blank somewhat. None of the dreams seemed to tell any "story." They were fixed and static, like tableaux or dioramas, solely designed, as it were, to exhibit their appalling-boring center-piece, this nothingness, this phantom, of which nothing could be said.

I would wake from them briefly—I must have had dozens that night—take a sip of water, turn on the light, and there, facing me, unchanged by waking, lay the chalky-blank reality, or unreality, of my dreams. It was in one of these wakings—the gritty intimations of dawn now showing through the window—that I suddenly realized that these were neurological dreams, not devoid of obsessive Freudian determinants, but centered on an unchanging organic determinant. And now I suddenly realized that, although I had never had such dreams myself before, I had sometimes heard of precisely such from my patients: patients with strokes, with paraplegias, with severe neuropathies—phantoms of amputees; patients with various pathologies and injuries, but all having in common severe disorders of body-image. What such patients would dream of, night after night—as indeed I was to do—was based precisely on their disorders of body-image, and the pseudo-images, the phantoms, which these engendered. My own dreams, it now seemed to me, confirmed precisely this—that part of my body-image, body-ego, had died a frigid death. Great alarm, and great relief, attended this conclusion, and forthwith I fell asleep again—into a deep and dreamless sleep, which gave way, towards morning, to a most singular nightmare, although it appeared, at first, to be no more than a "conventional" nightmare. We were at war—with whom, and why, was never too clear. What was clear, or on everyone's lips, was the fear that the

Enemy had an Ultimate Weapon, a so-called Derealization Bomb. It could, so it was whispered, *blow a hole in reality*. Ordinary weapons only destroyed matter extended through a certain space: *this* destroyed thought, and thought-space, itself. None of us knew what to think or expect, since, we had been told, the effect was unthinkable.

Like many people in my dream, I felt a need to be out in the open, and was standing with my family in our garden at home. The sun was shining, all seemed normal— except for the uncanny stillness about us. Suddenly I had a sense that something had happened, that something was beginning to happen, though what it was, I had no idea. I became aware that our pear-tree was missing. It was slightly to the left of where I was looking—and now, suddenly, there was no pear-tree, the pear-tree wasn't there!

I did not turn my head to investigate this further. For some reason, indeed, it did not occur to me to shift my gaze. The pear-tree was gone, but so was the place where the pear-tree stood. There was no sense of a place vacated; it was simply that the place was no longer there. No longer? Could I be sure that it *had* been there? Perhaps there was nothing missing. Perhaps there had never been a pear-tree there. Perhaps my memory or imagination was playing me a trick. I asked my mother, but she was as confounded as I was, and in just the same way: she too could no longer see the tree, but also doubted whether it had ever been there. Was this the derealization bomb at work, or were our apprehensions begetting ludicrous fancies?

And now part of the garden-wall was missing—including the gate which led on to Exeter Road. Or *was* it missing? Perhaps there had never been any garden-wall. Perhaps there had never been a gate which faced on to

Exeter Road, and no Exeter Road. *Perhaps there had never been anything whatever to the left?* My mother herself, who had moved so that she now stood straight ahead of me, seemed *bisected* in an extraordinary way. She stopped in the middle—she had no left half. But . . . but . . . could I be sure that she had a left half? Was not the very phrase "a left half" somehow meaningless? An extreme dread and nausea suddenly gripped me. I felt I would vomit. . . .

The door suddenly opened, and Nurse Sulu entered looking very concerned.

"I'm sorry for bursting in like this," she said, "but I peeped through the panel, and you looked terribly white, as though you were in shock. And your chest was heaving. I thought you were about to vomit. Do you feel all right?"

I nodded numbly, staring at her. "Why are you staring at me like that?" she asked.

"Oh . . . ummm . . . it's nothing," I said. "I just had a bad dream." I didn't care to tell Nurse Sulu, who had had enough shocks already, that *she* was bisected, and half of her was missing. And for those first waking seconds—or was I still half-asleep?—I had the strange feeling that, perhaps, she was complete as she was. I had remembered her saying, yesterday, that she was "only half-qualified," and for a moment I connected this with her appearance. And then, suddenly, with a most enormous and wonderful relief, I realized: I was having one of my migraines. *I had completely lost my visual field to the left, and with this, as would sometimes happen, the sense that there was (or had been, or could be) any world on the left.* My migraine *scotoma* had come on during sleep, and formed the physiological reality of the "derealization bomb" and the strange disappearance of the pear-tree, the garden-wall and the left half of my mother. And waking I had found this dream a reality, or rather what was real in the dream, and not merely staging, setting, symbolic, was equally real now that I was awake.

"But you *do* look very pale and sick," Nurse Sulu persisted, speaking quite normally despite having only half a face.

"Well, yes. I woke up with a migraine—one of my auras." I giggled. The half-vision, the *hemianopia*, seemed rather funny now I knew what it was, and that it would go away soon. "But I'll be all right soon. Maybe a nice cup of tea, and some toast, in a few minutes, when my stomach and my eyesight—" I giggled again—"has settled."

Reassured, Nurse Sulu turned to the door, regaining as she did so her unbisected form.

Yet knowing that I was hemianopic, with a super-added hemi-inattention for the affected side—knowing this, intellectually, did nothing to alter the hiatus in perception, or, rather, the hiatus in sense, the feeling that there *was* nothing other than what I saw, and that it was therefore senseless to look at, or look for, the "left" half of the room, so-called. With a violent effort of will, like a man forcing himself to move, inch by inch, in a nightmare, I turned my head towards the left. And there, thank God, there came into view the remainder of my bed, the half-covered window, the dim lithograph (showing Lord Lister, apparently, strangling a patient), the left wall of the room and—ah! nice to know I still had it—my left arm outflung on the pillow. Absurdly relieved at finding everything in its place, I turned my head slowly back to the straight forward position, amused at the gradual disappearance, once

again, of the left half of my visual field, the left half of
the room, the left half of the world, the idea of "leftness."

Yes! I could find it amusing, and instructive, *now*—
now that I knew what was going on, and that it was transient—but I had found it absolutely terrifying in my dream,
and in the first moments of waking, before I realized what
had happened. And as a child, I recollected, when I used
to get such attacks I found them inconceivably frightening. In those vulnerable years I became acutely sensitive
to two things: first, the least change or disorder in my
perceptions, and secondly, the dangers of "admitting" any
such change to the wrong people, in case they were regarded as "made-up" or "crazy."

These thoughts passed swiftly through my mind,
while I was still hemianopic, followed by a sudden pierc-
ing sense of analogy and insight: "Why, this is what's going
on with the leg! How could I be such a fool? I have
a *scotoma* for the leg! What I am experiencing with half
my visual field is essentially similar to what I am experiencing with my leg. I have lost the 'field' for my leg precisely
as I have lost part of my visual field."

I left an immense sense of relief as the thought became clear in my mind. It left all other sorts of questions
and uncertainties unresolved—including the rather crucial
question whether it would ever get better—but it gave me
a central support and insight to hold on to.

And now—yes—something was happening in the
blind half of my *scotoma*. A most delicate filigree pattern
had appeared while I mused, more delicate and transparent than the finest spider web, and with a sort of faint,
quivering, trembling, boiling motion. It became clearer,
brighter, a lattice of exquisite geometric beauty, composed,

I could now see, entirely of hexagons, and covering the whole half-field like gossamer lacework. The missing half of the room now grew visible, but remained entirely contained within the lacework, so that it appeared itself latticed in structure—a mosaic of hexagonal pieces, perfectly dovetailed and juxtaposed with each other. There was no sense of space, of solidity or extension, no sense of objects except as facets geometrically apposed, no sense of space and no sense of motion or time.

At this point, when I was relishing with a sort of detached, impersonal, mathematical interest this spaceless, motionless mosaic vision (which I had experienced, occasionally, before), Nurse Sulu entered with a cup of tea and toast. "You're looking *much* better," she said. "You look half-dead one minute and bright-eyed the next. I have never had such a changable patient."

I thanked her for the tea, which she put on my bedside table to the right, and then, impulsively, I asked if she had a minute.

"What now?" she smiled, thinking of my bizarre experiments the day before.

"Nothing much," I replied. "I won't ask you to *do* anything. But, if you would, could you go over to the other side of the room, by the window maybe, or by that sinister picture of Lord Lister?"

She crossed the room, suddenly being transformed as she did so, into a mosaic herself: there was an astounding moment, precisely in the middle, when one half of her was mosaic, and the other half *real*. She stood motionless by the window, backlit by the morning light which filtered through—and, in that moment, half-silhouetted, half-illuminated, her geometrized form in the embrasure of the window made me think of a madonna set in a medieval stained-glass window. Suddenly I felt frightened. She had become inorganic, part of the mosaic! How would I perceive movement, life, in this crystalline world?

I asked her to look at the picture, talk, gesture, make faces, anything, so long as she moved. And now, to my mixed delight and disquiet, I realized that time was fractured, no less than space, for I did not see her movements as continuous, but, instead, as a succession of "stills," a succession of different configurations and positions, but without any movement in-between, like the flickering of a film (the "flicks") run too slow. She seemed to be transfixed in this odd mosaic-cinematic state, which was essentially shattered, incoherent, atomized. And I couldn't imagine how this broken mosaic world could ever become one of continuity and coherence. I couldn't imagine—but, all of a sudden, it did! The mosaic, the flickering, were gone in an instant—and there was Nurse Sulu, no longer decomposed in space and time, but real and solid, warm and alive, quick, beautiful, once more in the stream of action and life. There had been beauty, mathematical beauty, in the crystalline world, but no beauty of action, no beauty of grace.

"That's it," I said with delight. "I think you helped to chase the aura away! And the nausea's all gone. Now—yes, *now*—I would like those kippers I smelt earlier."

I ate an enormous, a most sumptuous breakfast, much to the surprise of Nurse Sulu, who had seen me ashen-pale and retching less than an hour before. But after such attacks the patient "awakes a different being" (as the great Dr. Liveing wrote), and I indeed felt a different being, resurrected, reborn after my night of horrors and migraine.

But what made this rebirth even more joyous was the feeling that I had achieved by analogy some understanding of my "leg." This understanding had no effect on the physiological reality, but it took it out of the realms of the incomprehensible, the unmentionable—I could discuss it with Swan. He, I felt sure, would be deeply fascinated—and in turn could reassure me on the two points which now mattered: what had caused my *scotoma* and how long would it last? There were other questions I would like to put to him, if time permitted: how often did he see such *scotomata* in his practice, and were they well described in the medical literature? Yes, not only would I be given the reassurance I so badly needed, but I would have the chance of a fascinating exchange with my colleague, which would make clearer for us both this fascinating field on the borders of orthopedics and neurology.

I was so excited by the prospect, that I ate my huge breakfast in a state of abstraction, only subliminally appreciating the lovely crisp kippers.

In due course Sister came in.

"Look what a mess you are in, Dr. Sacks!" she said, in good-humored reproof. "You have books and letters and pieces of paper all round you—and, I do believe, you have spilt *ink* on the sheets!"

"It's my fountain pen," I apologized. "Sometimes it leaks."

"Well, we must get everything cleared up and ship-shape after breakfast. It's Grand Rounds today" (Sister's voice somehow seemed to capitalize the words) "and Mr. Swan will be here promptly at nine!"

With a smile, and a head-shake, she bounced out.

"She's a good sort," I thought, in my kipperish

euphoria. "A bit stern, a bit of a martinet, but a Sister must be that. She's a good-hearted old thing, under that rough voice, that awful exterior . . ."

My teapot was whisked away before my third cup, and Nurse Sulu brought me a basin, and whispered "Quick! Shave!"

I removed the untidy growth of six days—was it just six days since I set out on the Mountain?—and trimmed my beard. I cleaned my teeth and gargled.

Nurse Sulu helped me into the chair, put clean sheets on the bed and tidied the room. Then she helped me back into bed, saying: "Sister likes the patients propped up, right in the middle. Try and stay in the center. Don't lean to one side!"

I agreed to follow her instructions and asked her to leave the door open, because I had caught the sounds of the whole ward being cleared up and made shipshape— sounds so extraordinary that I wanted to hear them more clearly. Sister was barking, but good-humoredly, like a sergeant-major. The nurses and aides were running to-and-fro, all untidiness and litter were being softly abolished. There was the half-serious, half-comic sense of a military inspection—boots shined, puttees blancoed, chests out, stomachs in, everything ready and perfect.

The bustle, shouting and laughter was terrific. I was sorry I could only hear it, not see it. In the vast din everything was becoming orderly under the power of Sister's voice and eye. Now I saw us less as a parade-ground, more as a great ship being readied and made shipshape for something.

Suddenly the bustle and clatter seemed to cease, and was replaced by an extraordinary stillness. I heard a whispering, a murmuring, of which I could distinguish nothing.

And now Swan entered, accompanied by Sister bearing his surgical and ceremonial tools on a tray, followed by the Senior Registrar and his Juniors in long white coats. Finally came the Students, in short coats, looking unusually subdued. Formally and somberly as a religious procession, the chief and his retinue entered my room.

Swan neither looked at me nor greeted me, but took the chart which hung at the foot of my bed and looked at it closely.

"Well, Sister," he said, "and how is the patient now?"

"No fever, now, Sir," she answered. "We took the catheter out on Wednesday. He is taking food by mouth. There is no swelling of the foot."

"Sounds fine," said Mr. Swan, and then turned to me, or, rather, to the cast before me. He rapped it sharply with his knuckles.

"Well, Sacks," he said. "How does the leg seem today?"

"It seems fine, Sir," I replied, "surgically speaking."

"What do you mean—'surgically speaking'?" he said.

"Well, umm—" I looked at Sister, but her face was stony. "There's not much pain, and—er—there's no swelling of the foot."

"Splendid," he said, obviously relieved. "No problems then, I take it?"

"Well, just one." Swan looked severe, and I started to stammer. "It's . . . it's . . . I don't seem to be able to contract the quadriceps . . . and, er . . . the muscle doesn't seem to have any tone. And . . . and . . . I have difficulty locating the position of the leg."

I had a feeling that Swan looked frightened for a moment, but it was so momentary, so fugitive, that I could not be sure.

"Nonsense, Sacks," he said sharply and decisively. "There's nothing the matter. Nothing at all. Nothing to be worried about. Nothing at all!"

"But . . ."

He held up his hand, like a policeman halting traffic. "You're completely mistaken," he said with finality. "There's nothing wrong with the leg. You understand that, don't you?"

With a brusque and, it seemed to me, irritable movement, he made for the door, his Juniors parting deferentially before him.

I tried to catch the expression of the team as they turned, but their faces were closed and told me nothing. Swiftly the procession wheeled from the room.

I was stunned. All the agonized, agonizing uncertainties and fears, all the torment I had suffered since I discovered my condition, all the hopes and expectations I had pinned on this meeting—and now this! I thought: what sort of doctor, what sort of person, is this? He didn't even listen to me. He showed no concern. He doesn't listen to his patients—he doesn't give a damn. Such a man never listens to, never learns from, his patients. He dismisses them, he despises them, he regards them as nothing. And then I thought—I am being terribly unfair. I was provocative, unwittingly, when I said "surgically speaking." Further, we were both on the spot, because of the formality, the officialdom, of Grand Rounds. Both of us, in a sense, were forced to play roles—he the role of the All-knowing Specialist, I the role of the Know-nothing Patient.

And this was sharpened and made worse by my being, and being seen as, and partly acting as, his peer, so that neither of us really quite knew where we stood. And again; I could be certain that he was not really unfeeling—I had seen feeling, strong feeling, which he had to suppress, precisely as Miss Preston did when she saw the denervation. How different it might have been if we had met as individuals— but this was impossible in the grim context of Grand Rounds. Perhaps all would be different if I could have a quiet word with his Registrar—a cozy man-to-man chat after Grand Rounds.

The Staff-Nurse said "Yes," she would ask him to drop by. But the Registrar, alas, was exasperated and exasperating, obviously annoyed that I had asked for this special extra meeting.

"Well, Sacks," he snorted. "What's the matter now? Haven't you been told there is nothing the matter? Are you critical of the surgery or post-operative care?"

"Not at all," I replied. "Both seem exemplary."

"What *is* the matter then?"

"The leg doesn't *feel* right."

"This is very vague and subjective. Not the sort of thing we can be concerned with. We orthopods are really carpenters, in a way. We are called in to do a job. We do it. And that's that."

"Since you speak of carpentry," I replied, "That's just what it feels like. Carpentry would suffice if it were a wooden leg. And this *is* exactly how the leg feels—wooden, not like flesh, not alive, not mine."

"Sacks, you're unique," the Registrar said. "I've never heard anything like this from a patient before."

"I can't be unique," I said, with anger, and rising

panic. "I must be constituted the same way as everyone else! Perhaps (my anger was getting the better of me now), perhaps you don't listen to what patients say, perhaps you're not interested in the experiences they have." "No, indeed, I can't waste time with 'experiences' like this. I'm a practical man, I have work to do."

"Experience aside then, the leg doesn't *work*." "That's not my business."

"Then whose business is it? Specifically, there is something physiologically the matter. What about a neurological opinion, nerve-conduction tests, EMGs, etc.?"

He turned away and gave me no answer.*

---

* It was only four years later that I was put through nerve-conduction tests, electromyograms, and so forth. These showed that there was still quite severe denervation of the quadriceps, and marked impairment of conduction in the femoral nerve which supplies it. At the time of my "alienation," my *scotoma*, these impairments must have been profound —or absolute.

CHAPTER THREE

LIMBO

A land of darkness, as darkness itself—and of the shadow of death, without any order; and where the light is as darkness.
—Job 10:22

The *scotoma*, and its resonances, I had already experienced —frightful, empty images of nothingness, which surged, and overwhelmed me, especially at night. As a bulwark against this—I had hoped, and supposed—would come the genial understanding and support of my doctor. He would reassure me, help, give me a foothold in the darkness.

But, instead, he did the reverse. By saying nothing, saying "Nothing," he took away a foothold, the human foothold, I so desperately needed. Now, doubly, I had no leg to stand on; unsupported, doubly, I entered nothingness and Limbo.

The word "hell" supposedly is cognate with "hole"— and the hole of a *scotoma* is indeed a sort of hell: an existential, or metaphysical, state, indeed, but one with the clearest organic basis and determinant. The organic foundation of "reality" is removed, and to this extent one falls into a hole—or a hell-hole, if one permits oneself consciousness of this (which many patients, understandably, and defensively, do not do). A *scotoma* is a hole in reality itself, a hole in time no less than in space, and therefore *cannot* be conceived of as having a term or ending. As it carries a quality of "memory-hole," of amnesia, so it carries a sense of timelessness, endlessness. The quality of timelessness, Limbo, is inherent in *scotoma*.

This would be tolerable, or more tolerable, if it could be communicated to others, and become a subject of understanding and sympathy—like grief. This was denied me when the surgeon said "Nothing," so that I was thrown into the further hell—the hell of communication denied.

> This is the secret delight, the security of Hell [the Devil says, in *Dr. Faustus*] that it is not to be informed on, that it is protected from speech, that it cannot be made public. . . . Soundlessness, forgottenness, hopelessness, are poor weak symbols. *Here everything leaves off.* . . . No man can hear his own tune.

A sense of utter hopelessness swept over me.

I felt myself sinking. The abyss engulfed me. Although *scotoma* means "shadow" or "darkness"—and this is the usual symbolism of horror and death—I was sensorially and spiritually more affected by silence. I kept reading *Dr. Faustus* at this time, especially its passage on Hell—and Music. "No man can hear his own tune," on the one hand; on the other the noise, the infernal din of hell. And this was literalized in the roomless room, the cell, where I lay, in the privation of music, and the pressure of noise. I yearned—hungrily, thirstily, desperately—for music, but my rotten little radio could pick up almost nothing, the buildings, the scaffolding, almost barring reception. And, on the other hand, there were pneumatic drills the whole day, as work was done on the scaffolding a few feet from my ears. Outwardly, then, there was soundlessness and noise, and inwardly, simultaneously, a deadly inner silence—the silence of timelessness, motionlessness, *scotoma*, combined with the silence of non-communication and taboo. Incommunicable, *incommunicado*, the sense of excommunication was extreme. I maintained an affable and amenable surface, while nourishing an inward and secret despair.

"If you stare into the abyss," wrote Nietzsche, "it will stare back at you."

The abyss is a chasm, an infinite rift, in reality. If you but notice it, it may open beneath you. You must either turn away from it, or face it, fair and square. I am very tenacious, for better or worse. If my attention is engaged, I cannot disengage it. This may be a great strength, or weakness. It makes me an investigator. It makes me an obsessional. It made me, in this case, an *explorer* of the abyss. . . .

I had always liked to see myself as a naturalist or explorer. I had explored many strange, neuropsychological lands—the furthest Arctics and Tropics of neurological disorder. But now I decided—or was I forced?—to explore a chartless land. The land which faced me was No-land, Nowhere.

All the cognitive and intellectual and imaginative powers which had previously aided me in exploring different neuropsychological lands were wholly useless, meaningless, in the limbo of Nowhere. I had fallen off the map, the world, of the knowlable. I had fallen out of space, and out of time too. Nothing could happen, ever, any more. Intelligence, reason, sense, meant nothing. Memory, imagination, hope, meant nothing. I had lost everything which afforded a foothold before. I had entered, willy-nilly, a dark night of the soul.

This involved, first, a very great fear. For I had to relinquish all the powers I normally command. I had to relinquish, above all, the sense and affect of *activity*. I had to allow—and this seemed horrible—the sense and feeling of *passivity*. I found this humiliating, at first, a mortification of my self—the active, masculine, ordering self, which I had equated with my science, my self-respect, my mind. And then, mysteriously, I began to change—to allow, to welcome this abdication of activity. I began to perceive this change on the third day of Limbo.

To the soul, lost, confounded in the darkness, the long night, neither charts, nor the chart-making mind, were of service. Nor, indeed, was the *temper* of the charter— "strong masculine sense . . . enterprise . . . vigilance and activity" (as a contemporary wrote of Captain Cook). These active qualities might be valuable later, but at this point they had nothing to work on. For my state in the dark night was one of passivity, an intense and absolute and essential passivity, in which action—any action—would be useless and distraction. The watchword at this time was "Be patient—endure. . . . Wait, be still. . . . Do nothing, don't think!" How difficult, how paradoxical, a lesson to learn!

> Be still, and wait without hope
> For hope would be hope of the wrong thing; wait
>   without love

For love would be love of the wrong thing . . .
Wait without thought, for you are not ready for
    thought . . .

                        —Eliot

I had to be still, and wait in the darkness, to feel it as holy, the darkness of God, and not simply as blindness and bereftness (though it entailed, indeed, total blindness and bereftness). I had to acquiesce, even be glad, that my reason was confounded, and that my powers and faculties had no locus of action and could not be exerted to alter my state. I had not sought this, but it had happened, and so I should accept it—accept this strange passivity and night, this strange *scotoma* of the senses and reason, not with anger, not with terror, but with gratitude and gladness.

This, then, was the change, starting on the third day of my Limbo, which moved me from a sense of abomination and despair, a sense of a hideous and unspeakable hell, to a sense of something utterly, mysteriously, different—a night no longer abominable and dark, but radiant, secretly, with a light above sense—and, with this, a curious, paradoxical joy:

> In darkness and secure, By the secret ladder, disguised—ah, happy chance!
> In Darkness and concealment, my House being now at rest.
> In the happy night, in secret, where none saw me,
> Nor I beheld aught. Without light or guide, save that which burned in my heart.
> This light guided me. More surely than the light of noonday to the place where He was awaiting me . . .

                    —St. John of the Cross

I had thought, in the pride of reason, in the noonday light of reason, that whatever was worth accomplishing in life could be accomplished by reason and will, by that "strong masculine sense . . . enterprise . . . vigilance and activity" which had previously characterized my endeavors. Now, for the first time in my life perhaps, I had tasted, been forced to taste, something quite different—to experience, in patienthood, the profoundest passivity; and to realize that this was the only proper attitude at the time . . .

Socially I had to try to be active and adult, and avoid more than the minimum necessary dependence on others; but spiritually—which was not socially, but inwardly—I had to relinquish all my powers and pretensions, all my adult, masculine enterprise and activity, and be childlike, patient, and passive, in the long night, this being the only proper posture of the soul at this time. I had to wait, to be still—for He was awaiting me . . .

The captain of the plane, a bluff hearty man, full of enterprise and decision and strong masculine sense, even he had said, had he not: "The first thing about being a patient is—to be patient"; and, earlier in my hospital stay, one of the surgical registrars (alas, not my own), seeing me vexed, irritable, impatient, and fretting, had said gently: "Take it easy! The whole thing, going through it, is really a pilgrimage."

Thus my limbo—which lasted for a timeless twelve days—started as torment, but turned into patience; started as hell, but became a purgatorial dark night; humbled me, horribly, took away hope, but, then, sweetly-gently, returned it to me a thousandfold, transformed.

In this limbo, when I journeyed to despair and back— a journey of the soul, for my medical circumstances were unchanged, arrested in the motionless fixity of *scotoma*, and in an agreement, not uncordial, between my physicians and myself not to make any reference to "deeper things"— in this limbo, this dark night, I could not turn to science. Faced with a reality, which reason could not solve, I turned to art and religion for comfort. It was these, and these only, that could call through the night, could communicate, could make sense, make more intelligible—and tolerable: "We have art, in order that we may not perish from the truth" (Nietzsche).

Science and reason could not talk of "nothingness," of "hell," of "limbo"; or of spiritual "night." They had no place for "absence, darkness, death." Yet these were the overwhelming realities of this time. I turned to the Bible— especially the Psalms—because these continually spoke of such things, and of a return, mysteriously, to light and life once again. I turned to them as descriptions, as "case-histories," in a way, but also with hope, as a sort of prayer or invocation. And I turned to the mystics, and the Metaphysical poets too, for they also offered both formulation and hope—poetic, esthetic, metaphoric, symbolic, without the blunt plain commitment that "religion" involved.

> Study me then, you who shall lovers be
> At the next world, that is, at the next spring
> For I am every dead thing,
> In whom love wrought new alchemie.
> For his art did expresse
> A quintessence even from nothingnesse,
> From dull privations, and lean emptinesse,
> He ruin'd me, and I am rebegot,
> Of Absence, Darknesse, Death; things which are
> not.
>
> —Donne

Donne's midwinter ode, from a midwinter of life, com-municated to me the plight, and hope, of the dead soul. I often murmured it to myself, especially the last words: "I am rebegot / of Absence, Darknesse, Death; things which are not." Or, sometimes, just "I am, I will be, rebegot." I repeated them in a sort of litany or soliloquy. I hugged them, and held them, closer and closer to me, for they seemed to hint at some secret, impossible hope, where I could see no reason to hope.

But finally, the Metaphysicals and mystics were laid aside, and there remained only the Scriptures, the im-possible faith:

> Thou, which hast shewed me great and sore troubles, shalt quicken me again, and shalt bring me up from the depths of the earth.
>
> —Psalms 71:20

Secretly, half-skeptically, hesitantly, yearningly, I ad-dressed myself to this unimaginable "Thou."

CHAPTER FOUR

QUICKENING

But by what means may the animal be moved by inward principles . . . ? By means of what instruments? . . . let us compare *automata* . . . Is the first instrument of movement spirit? Or natural causes—like the movement of the heart?
—William Harvey, *De Motu Locali Animalium*

Throughout these twelve, endless yet empty days the leg itself had not changed a jot; it remained entirely motionless, toneless, senseless, beneath its white sepulchre of chalk. Its absolute fixity and unchangability, its replacement, so to speak, by an inorganic white cylinder, its lifeless, petrified and calcarious quality, were re-presented to me every night, countless times a night. And my dreams —these too changed not a jot, but retained the same eidetic and diagrammatic vividness, the same absence of any motion, or happening, or event, the same deadness, as they had exhibited on their first appearance.

The *idea* of any progress, any change, or any hint or hope of this, was continually nulled and annulled until the following Saturday morning. I quote the following entry from my Diary:

> New phenomena from leg. Sudden, incredibly severe, extremely brief flashes of pain from somewhere in the leg, strobe-like in their blinding intensity and brevity. "Lightning pains" are similar. . . . Such a pain absolutely convulses one while it lasts, but its duration is only a few thousandths of a second. I wonder about the physiology of these extraordinary pain flashes. What *on earth goes on?*
>
> I have also started to have involuntary flash-like twitches in the previously inert and silent muscle. Both the twitches and the flashes are almost spinal in quality, as if isolated sensory or motor cells are involved. . . .
>
> They give a double feeling—part fear, part hope. They are obviously pathological. Their character indicates that a genuine denervation is involved. But their very appearance is perhaps a sign of returning innervation.
>
> No voluntary movement is yet possible or thinkable, but these involuntary flashes—fulgurations and fasciculations—are perhaps the first sparks of life—and may indicate that the muscle is getting *ready* to respond.

These fasciculations of the muscle, not at all "private," but perfectly visible to all, represented the first positive reality since I had entered the hospital. These crackles and flashes were a token and earnest of neurological recovery, a sign that some irritability, some "life," was coming back to the nerve-muscle, since its injury two weeks before. They gave me a strong sense of electrical activity—a sort of spontaneous "faradization" or fulguration of nerve-muscle—an electrical kindling of the tardy spark of life. . . .

I had very much the feeling of an electrical storm—of

lightning flashes jumping from one fiber to another, and an electrical muttering and crackling in the nerve-muscle. I could not help being reminded of Frankenstein's monster, connected up to a lightning rod, and crackling to life with the flashes.

I felt, then, on Saturday, that I was "electrified" or rather, that a small and peripheral part of the nervous system was being electrified into life: not me, *it*. . . . I played no part in these local, involuntary flashes and spasms. They were nothing to do with *me*, my will. They did not go with any feeling of intention or volition, nor with any idea of movement. They neither stimulated, nor were stimulated by, idea or intention; thus they conveyed no *personal* quality; they were not voluntary, not *actions* —just sporadic flashes at the periphery—none the less a clear and crucial and most welcome sign that whatever had happened, or had been happening, peripherally, was now starting to show some return of function—abnormal, flash-like, paroxysmal function, but any function was better than no function at all.

Throughout Limbo I yearned for music, but was frustrated in my efforts to obtain it. By mid-week I was sick of my impossible radio, and asked a friend if he would bring in a tape-recorder and music. On Saturday morning—that same Saturday, the 7th—he brought along his recorder with a single cassette, saying he was sorry, this was the only one he could find. It was Mendelssohn's Violin Concerto.

I had never been a special Mendelssohn lover, although I had always enjoyed the liveliness and exquisite lightness of his music. It was (and remains) a matter of amazement to me that this charming, trifling piece of music should have had such a profound and, as it turned out, decisive effect on me. From the moment the tape started, from the first bars of the Concerto, something happened, something of the sort I had been panting and thirsting for, something that I had been seeking more and more frenziedly with each passing day, but which had eluded me. Suddenly, wonderfully, I was moved by the music. The music seemed passionately, wonderfully, quiveringly alive —and conveyed to me a sweet feeling of life. I felt, with the first bars of the music, a hope and an intimation that life would return to my leg—that *it* would be stirred, and stir, with original movement, and recollect or recreate its forgotten motor melody. I felt—how inadequate words are for feelings of this sort!—I felt, in those first heavenly bars of music, as if the animating and creative principle of the whole world was revealed, that life itself was music, or consubstantial with music; that our living moving flesh, itself, was "solid" music—music made fleshy, substantial, corporeal. In some intense, passionate, almost mystical sense, I felt that music, indeed, might be the cure to my problems—or, at least, a key of an indispensable sort.

I played the Concerto again and again. I didn't tire of it: I desired nothing else. Every playing was a refreshment and a renewal of my spirit. Every playing seemed to open new vistas. Was music, I wondered, the very *score* of life—the key, the promise, of renewed action and life?

On Saturday and Sunday—weekend of hope!—the sense of hopelessness, of interminable darkness, lifted. I had a sense—not of dawn, but the first intimations of dawn: it was still mid-winter, but a spring might perhaps come. How, I didn't know—it could not be conceived, it was not a matter which could be solved (even touched) by conjecture or thought. It was not a problem but a mystery which I faced—the mystery of a new beginning and quickening. Perhaps there had to be, before this, an infinite darkness and silence. Perhaps this was the womb, the night-womb, in which new life was created.

Not only was there some lifting of the hopelessness that weekend, but a curious sort of lightness and gaiety of spirit. There was the sense of a possible convalescence. A sense of renewal grew upon me.

Each time I played the Mendelssohn, on the recorder, or in my mind, and each time I had a sudden electric spasm of the muscle, this spirit of hope took hold of me again. Yet, my hope was, in some sense, theoretical—it was not clear that I had anything to be hopeful about. I still thought of the leg, of the flesh, as "finished." What was music, what were these fine feelings, if I lacked the mechanism, the apparatus, the flesh? I desperately needed to see the leg—to see that its substance, its flesh, its reality, was intact. And by good fortune and timing, this was to occur the next day.

On Monday morning, the fourteenth day after surgery, I was due to go down to the Casting Room, to have the wound inspected and the stitches removed. In these two weeks, indeed since the night of the accident, I had not actually been able to see the leg—it had always been covered and encased in a cast. There was something about the cast—its smooth featurelessness, it sepulchral whiteness, and its shape, which was like a vague and obscene parody of a leg—which invested it with horror: and indeed, as such, it played a great role in my dreams.

The night before I was due to be taken down, and

uncasted, these dreams rose to a frightful climax: I dreamed, woke briefly, fell into the same dreams—hundreds of times I must have dreamt of the cast as empty, or solid all through, or filled with a disgusting verminous mass of rotting bones, bugs and pus. The Mendelssohnian joy, and mirth, and gaiety, had all gone. When the dim gray dawn of Monday finally came, I felt shuddery and weak, too sick to have breakfast, to say anything, or think. I lay like a corpse in my bed, waiting to be carried out.

The very term "casting room" had a grim and frightful resonance. Even the word "cast" took on disquieting other meanings. I found unbidden images rising in my mind—of the Casting Room as a place where they cast and cast away; where new limbs and bodies were cast by the Caster, and old and useless ones were cast away. Such fancies kept bursting into my mind, and I could not dismiss them, absurd though they were.

It was a relief, but also a terror, when the orderlies finally came for me and heaved me on a stretcher and out of the room. Out of my room! For the first time in fifteen days. I caught a brief glimpse of the sky as we waited to go down. The sky! I had forgotten it, forgotten the outside world, as I lay in my small windowless cell, in solitary confinement, excited, obsessed, my mind a pressure-cooker of thoughts. The rumbling of the stretcher-trolley seemed monstrously loud, and kept suggesting to me the roll of tumbrils, the sense of being taken to my death—or something worse than death: to the realization of an abominable nightmare, where all my fantasies of the uncanny, the unalive, the unreal, would turn out true.

The Casting Room was small, white, featureless,

somewhere between a surgery and a workshop, with shears and other implements hanging on the wall—the strange, frightening tools of the Caster's Art. The orderlies shifted me on to a raised block in the center—something between a catafalque and a butcher's block, I felt—and went out, shutting the door behind them. I was suddenly alone in this uncanny silent room.

And then I realized that I was not alone. The Caster, in a white gown, was standing in a corner. I had somehow failed to notice him when I was wheeled in. Or, perhaps, he had come in without my noticing. For, in a curious way, he did not seem to move, but to materialize suddenly in different parts of the room. He was here, he was there, but I never caught him in transit. He had a strangely immobile, carven face, with features of a medieval drawing. It might have been the face of Dürer, or of a mask or gargoyle imagined by Dürer.

I summoned up a social manner and said, "Hello, Mr. Enoch. Funny weather we're having."

He made no response—not a movement, not a flicker.

I made some further desultory comments, and then tailed off as he made no reply but continued to stand motionless in the corner with his arms folded and his eyes fixed on mine. I found myself increasingly unnerved—it crossed my mind that he might be mad.

And then, suddenly, without any intermediate movement, he was no longer in his corner, but by the wall where the shears and other tools hung. And now, in a flash, he had the shears in his hands. They looked monstrously large to me—and he looked vast too. I felt that with a single cut he could shear off my leg, or slice me in two.

A single bound and he was on me, shears wide open, for the first cut. I wanted to yell "Help! someone, anyone, come in! I am being attacked by a madman with a pair of shears." My reason told me that this was all fancy, that Mr. Enoch might be a little odd and taciturn, but was assuredly a skilled and responsible craftsman. So I controlled myself, and smiled, and said not a word.

And then I heard a reassuring sound—a gentle crunching, as the cast was snipped open. There had not been any terrible attack! Mr. Enoch was quietly doing his business. He slit open the cast from top to bottom, and then gently pulled it open, exposing the leg. The cast itself he tossed lightly in a corner. This astounded me, for I had imagined it was enormously heavy, forty or fifty pounds at the least. Friends, at my request, had lifted the two legs, and said "Blimey! That one in plaster weighs a ton—at least forty pounds heavier than the other one." From the way Mr. Enoch held it up and flicked it in a corner, it evidently weighed almost nothing at all, and the dead weight of the leg, that extra forty pounds, must have been due entirely to its total lack of muscular tone—that normal postural tone which one finds even in the deepest relaxation or sleep.

Mr. Enoch stepped back, or, rather, suddenly disappeared, and reappeared as suddenly in his original corner, with a faint enigmatic smile on his lips.

And now Sister and the Surgical Registrar came bustling in, smiling and chatting as if nothing had happened—nothing *had* happened.

Sister said she was going to remove the stitches, but the Registrar interposed: "Don't you want to *look* at your leg? After all, you haven't seen it for more than two weeks!"

Did I? Most assuredly, and passionately and eagerly; and yet I feared, shrinking, not knowing what I would see; and admixed with both feelings was a curious lack of feeling—a sort of indifference, real or defensive—so that I hardly cared what I would see.

With the Registrar's help, I raised myself on one arm, and took a long, long look at the leg.

Yes, it was there! Indisputably there! The cast was neither empty nor solid, as I had feared, nor did it contain a mass of earth, or dung, or rotting chicken bones. It contained—a leg, of approximately normal dimensions, though greatly wasted in comparison with its fellow, and with a long, clean scar about a foot long. A leg—and yet, not a leg: there was something all wrong. I was profoundly reassured, and at the same time disquieted, shocked, to the depths. For though it was "there"—it was not really there.

It was indeed "there" in a sort of formal, factual sense: visually there, but not livingly, substantially, or "really" there. It wasn't a real leg, not a real thing at all, but a mere semblance which lay there before me. I was struck by the beautiful, almost translucent, delicacy of the limb; and I was struck by its absolute, almost appalling, unreality. It was exquisite, lifeless, like a fine wax model from an anatomy museum.

Gingerly I put out my hand to touch it—and touch was as uncanny and equivocal as sight. It not only looked like wax, but it felt like wax—finely molded, inorganic and ghostly. I could not feel the feeling fingers with the leg, so I squeezed the leg, pinched it, pulled out a hair. I could have stuck a knife into it for all the feeling it had. There was absolutely no sensation whatever—I might have been squeezing and kneading lifeless dough. It was clear that I had a leg which looked anatomically perfect, and which had been expertly repaired, and healed without complication, but it looked and felt uncannily alien—a lifeless replica attached to my body. I thought again of the young man on that long-past New Year's Eve, his pale, scared face, and the consternation as he whispered: "It's just a counterfeit. It's not real. It's not mine."

"Well," said the Registrar. "You're looking hard enough. What do you think of it? We did a nice job, eh?"

"Yes, yes," I replied, bemusedly trying to gather my thoughts. "You did a very nice job, beautiful, really beautiful. I do thank and congratulate you. But—."

"Well, what's the 'but'?" he asked with a smile.

"It looks fine—it *is* fine, surgically speaking."

"What do you mean—'surgically speaking'?"

"Well, it doesn't *feel* right. It feels—sort of funny, not right, not mine. Difficult to put into words."

"Don't worry, old chap," the Registrar said. "It's done beautifully, old fellow. You'll be right as rain. Sister will take the stitches out now."

Sister advanced, with her gleaming instrument tray, saying, "It shouldn't hurt too much, Dr. Sacks. You'll probably just feel a tweaking sensation. If it does hurt we can put in some local."

"You go ahead," I answered. "I'll let you know if it hurts."

But, to my surprise, she didn't seem to be going ahead, but fiddling around, with her scissors and forceps—fiddling in the strangest, most unintelligible way. I watched her, perplexed, for a time and then closed my eyes. When I opened them, she had stopped her unconscionable fiddling, which, I suppose, must have been some sort of "warm-up" or preparatory activity: I presumed she was now ready to take out the stitches.

"You going to start now?" I enquired.

She looked at me in astonishment. "Start!" she exclaimed. "Why, I just finished! I took out all the stitches. I must say, you were very good. You lay quiet as a lamb. You must be very stoical. Did it hurt much?"

"No," I answered. "It didn't hurt at all. And I wasn't being brave. I didn't feel you at all. I had no sensation whatever when you pulled the stitches out." I omitted to say, because I thought it would sound too strange, that I had entirely failed to realize that she *was* taking them out, indeed that I had failed to make any sense of her activity whatever, or to see it as having any sense or relation to me, so that I had mistaken all her motions as meaningless "fiddling." But I was taken aback, confounded, by the business. It brought home to me once more how estranged the leg was, how "alien," how "exiled" from myself. To think that I could have seen Sister making all the characteristic motions of snipping and pulling out stitches, but was only able to imagine she was "warming up" in readiness for the "real thing"! Her activity had seemed meaningless and unreal, presumably, because the leg felt meaningless and unreal. And because the leg felt senseless, in all senses of senseless, absolutely senseless and unrelated to me, so had her motions which had been related to it. As the leg was merely a semblance, so her motions, her taking-out stitches, seemed merely a semblance. Both had been reduced to meaningless semblance.

Finding my horrible fears and phantasms unfounded, finding the leg at least formally intact and there, finding finally an infinite reassurance when Mr. Enoch lifted the heel off the block, and the knee locked firmly, precisely, in place, and that the horror of kneelessness, dislocation, disarticulation, was gone—I suddenly felt an infinite relief: a relief so sweet and intense, so permeating my whole being, that I was bathed in bliss. With this sudden sweet and profound reassurance, the sudden and profound change of mood, the leg was utterly transformed, transfigured. It still looked profoundly strange and unreal. It still looked profoundly unalive. But where it had previously brought to mind a corpse, it now made me think of a fetus, not yet born. The flesh seemed somehow translucent and innocent, like flesh not yet given the breath of life.

Theoretical as yet, the flesh was there, healed anatomically, but not yet quickened into action. It lay there patient, radiant, not yet real, but almost ready to be born. The sense of dreadful, irretrievable loss was transformed into a sense of mysterious "abeyance." It lay there, in a strange suspension, or limbo, a mysterious landscape between death and birth. . . .

. . . between two worlds, one dead
The other powerless to be born
     —Arnold

Flesh which was still as unliving as marble but, like the marble flesh of Galatea, might come to life. And even the new plaster partook of this feeling: I had hated the old one, feeling it putrid, obscene, but I immediately took a liking to the new one which Mr. Enoch was now carefully applying, laying layer upon layer round my new pink leg. This cast I thought elegant, shapely, even smart. More important, I thought of it as a sort of good chrysalis, which would sheathe the leg and let it develop completely, until it was ready to hatch, to be reborn.

As I was wheeled back from the Casting Room, and up in the elevator, we paused by the broad windows, which were open now to the air. The sky had been dark and charged before; but now the storm had broken, and it was heavenly calm and clear. I left the very elements themselves had had their crisis at precisely the same time as I had had mine. All was resolved now, the heavens clear and blue. A lovely breeze came through the great windows, and I felt intoxicated as the sun and wind played on my skin. It was my first sense of the outside world in more than two weeks, two weeks in which I had moldered, in despair, in my cell. And there was music, a new radio, when I returned to my room—wonderful Purcell, *Dido and Aeneas*—and this too, like the wind and the sun and the light, came like a heavenly refreshment to my senses. I felt bathed in the music, penetrated by it, healed and quickened through and through: divine music, spirit, message and messenger of life!

Relieved of all my anxieties and tensions, sure and confident that the leg would come back, and that I would recover and walk again—though when, and how, God only knew—I suddenly fell into a deep blissful sleep: sleeping in trust, cradled in God's arms. A deep, deep, and in itself healing, sleep—my first proper rest since the day of the accident—my first sleep uninterrupted by hideous nightmares and phantoms. The sleep of innocence, of forgiveness, of faith and hope renewed.

When I awoke I had an odd impulse to flex my left leg, and in that self-same moment immediately did so! Here was a movement previously impossible, one which involved active contraction of the whole quad—a movement hitherto impossible and unthinkable. And yet, in a trice, I had thought it, and done it. There was no cogitation, no preparation, no deliberation, whatever; there was no "trying"; I had the impulse, flash-like—and flash-like I acted. The idea, the impulse, the action, were all one—I could not say which came first, they all came together. I suddenly "recollected" how to move the leg, and in the instant of recollection I actually did it. The knowing-what-to-do had no theoretical quality whatever—it was entirely practical, immediate—and compelling. It came to me suddenly and spontaneously—out of the blue.

Excited, I rang my bell and called for the Nurse.

"Look!" I exclaimed. "I did it, I can do it!"

But when I tried to show her, nothing happened at all. The knowledge, the impulse, had departed as it came, suddenly, mysteriously. Mortified, and puzzled, I returned to my book—and then about half an hour later, and again in mid-word, unbidden, unconsidered, I had the same impulse again. The impulse, the idea, the remembrance, flashed back—and I moved my leg (if "moved" is not too deliberate a word for the utterly *un*deliberated, spontaneous movement which "occurred"). But a few seconds later it was impossible again. And so it was throughout the rest of the day. The power of moving, the idea of moving, the impulse to move, would suddenly come to me—and as suddenly go—as a word, or a face, or a name, or a tune, can be at the tip of one's tongue, or in the immediate ambit of one's vision or hearing, and then, as suddenly, disappear. Power was returning, but it was still labile, unstable, not yet securely fixed in my nervous system or mind. I was beginning to remember, but the memory came and went. I suddenly knew, and then didn't know—like an aphasic with words.

The term "ideomotor" came spontaneously to mind. The flashes I had had previously were merely motor, fragmentary spasms and twitches of an irritable nerve-muscle —there being no correspondence with any inner impulse, idea or intention. They had nothing to do with *me*— whereas these flashes, by contrast, involuntary, spontaneous, unbidden, as they were, did most certainly, and essentially, and fundamentally, involve *me*: they weren't just "a muscle jumping," but "*me* remembering," and they involved me, my mind, no less than my body. Indeed, they united my mind and my body; they exemplified, in a flash, their quintessential unity—the unity which had been lost, since my disconnecting injury.

The surgeon's original words recurred to me, "You'd been disconnected. We reconnect you. That's all." What he meant, in a purely local and anatomical sense, had, I now felt, a much vaster (if unintended) sense—the sense in which E. M. Forster says "Only connect." For what was disconnected was not merely nerve and muscle but, in consequence of this, the natural and innate unity of body and mind. The "will" was unstrung, precisely as the nerve-muscle. The "spirit" was ruptured, precisely as the body. Both were split, and split off from one another. And, since "body" and "soul" have sense only insofar as they are one, both became senseless when they no longer connected. In these ideomotor flashes, then, a most momentous reconnection, or re-union, occurred, even if it lasted no more than a moment—the convulsive reunion of body and soul.

Yet there was an extreme limitation, a peculiarity, to this will. First, it was good for nothing except a single, rather stereotyped, movement at the hip—and what sort of will has a repertoire of one movement? Secondly, it was always accompanied by an "impulse" or "impulsion"—of an oddly intrusive and irrelevant sort. I would be reading —in mid-sentence, my mind far away, utterly remote from anything to do with my leg—when all-of-a-sudden there would come this peremptory, and specific, impulsion. I welcomed it, enjoyed it, played with it—and finally mastered it. But it was will and action of a most peculiar sort, the resultant being a strange hybrid—half jerk, half act.

Recently I had to have—as the surgeon had originally suggested for the quadriceps—some electrical stimulation, to some injured neck muscles. Every time the current stimulated the trapezius muscles in the neck I had a sudden impulse to shrug my shoulders, to shrug them expressively, in the gesture "So?" It would occur to me to shrug my shoulders, as it might occur to anyone; except that the occurring only occurred when the trapezius was faradized. I found this experience amusing, fascinating—and some-what shocking; for it showed, very clearly, that one could have a sense or an illusion of free-will, even when the impulse was primarily physiological in nature. At such times, in effect, *one was no more than a puppet*—com-pelled to react, but imagining that the reaction was free. This, I now believe, was what had been happening with the strange half-convulsive, pseudo-voluntary contractions. I think that there were random sparks, or firings, of the now-recovering neuromuscular apparatus, which had been inactive, perhaps in a state of shock, since the surgery. Over the weekend, these firings were very small, very local, and caused only small fasciculations or flashes in individual muscle bundles. On Tuesday there started convulsive, massive jumps of the whole muscle (including its pelvic attachment) in such a way as to jerk the leg. These massive contractions—like the massive contractions of nocturnal myoclonus, or tics, or the massive contractions of a faradized trapezii or even knee-jerks—constituted a sort of short-circuit in, or stimulus to, the whole voluntary system. And, apparently, one cannot have a substantial portion of voluntary muscle activated, however mechanically or involuntarily, without stimulating (or simulating) a feeling of *voluntas*, of will. (This queer, quasi-voluntary feeling may occur when a patellar reflex (or "knee-jerk") is elicited.)

Perhaps one needs to distinguish different sorts of will—a passive-compulsive and an active-deliberative—but one may take over the passive-compulsive. Thus, in the course of that day, what started as puppet-like jerkings, and coercions, of the will, were transformed into active, controlled acts of will. The irritable innervation, returning to life, provided its own electric shocks; these, in turn, led to convulsive-compulsive, or tic-like, movements of the limb; and these, in their turn, to genuine voluntary acts.

All this was, in a sense, the reverse of the *scotoma*. There, it seemed to me, I willed—and nothing happened: so that I was forced into a singular doubt, and kept asking myself "Did I will? Have I will? What has happened to my will?" Now, suddenly, unbidden, out of the blue, I had sudden compulsions, or convulsions, of will.

And yet, ironically, this inversion, or perversion, or subversion, of will was precisely the means by which a recovery was effected. An accident of physiology, an injury, had deprived me of will—specifically and solely in relation to the injured limb; and now another accident of physiology, the sparks of returning innervation, were to rekindle will in this limb. First I was will-less, unable to command; then I was willed, or commanded, like a puppet; and now, finally, I could take over the reins of command, and say "I will" (or "I won't") with full truth and conviction, albeit in the single matter of moving my leg.

Wednesday the 11th had been set as The Day—the appointed day for me to arise, and stand, and walk. For the first time since my accident I would assume, it was to be hoped, the erect position—and erectness is moral, existential, no less than physical. For two weeks, for eighteen days, I had been prostrate, recumbent: doubly so—physically, through weakness and inability to stand; morally, through passivity, the posture of a *patient*—a man reduced, and dependent on his doctor.

The posture, the passivity of the patient lasts as long as the doctor orders, and its end cannot be envisaged until the very moment of rising. And this moment cannot be anticipated, or even thought of, even hoped for. One cannot see, one cannot conceive, beyond the limits of one's bed. One's mentality becomes wholly that of the bed, or the grave.

Until the actual moment of rising, it is as if one were never to arise: one is condemned (so one feels) to eternal prostration.

> I cannot rise out of my bed till the physician enable me, nay, I cannot tell that I am able to rise till he tells me so. I do nothing, I know nothing of myself. . . .

And if this was so for Donne, if this is so for every patient who is condemned to lie in bed ("miserable, and *though common to all*, inhuman posture . . ."), how much more so was it for me, given the peculiar and specific character of my own disorder, the sense of amputation, leglessness, of nothing to stand on. . . .

Rising, standing, walking pose for every bedridden patient a fundamental challenge, for he has forgotten, or been "disallowed," the adult, human posture and motions of uprightness, that physical-and-moral posture which means standing-up, standing-up-for-oneself, walking, and walking-away—walking away from one's physicians and parents, walking away from those upon whom one depended and hung, walking freely, and boldly, and adventurously, wherever one wishes.

To this universal was added the specific—that I had come to question the integrity, the very existence, of my leg, and that there was ground for this strange questioning in the actual injury of the leg. Especial and extraordinary difficulties exist for those not merely recumbent but also leg-injured; and these were precisely and pungently expressed by Hippocrates, two and a half thousand years ago. Speaking of patients who had suffered a broken hip, and had had to be immobilized in bed for a period of fifty days, this combination, he observed, "subdues the imagination, so that such patients cannot imagine how to move the leg, much less how to stand; and if they are not made to do so, will remain in bed for the rest of their lives." I had indeed to be made to rise, and stand, and walk—but how could I do so, and what indeed might happen, in a case such as mine, where to all the usual fears, inhibitions, hesitations, was superadded a fundamental disruption and "dissolution" of the leg, a disruption and dissolution at once physiological and existential?

Had ever I faced a more paradoxical situation? How could I stand, without a leg to stand on? How could I walk, when I lacked legs to walk with? How could I act, when the instrument of action had been reduced to an inert, immobile, lifeless, white thing?

What I kept thinking of, in particular, was a remarkable chapter in A. R. Luria's *The Man with a Shattered World*—a chapter entitled "The Turning Point." This was, in essence, for the patient, the recovery of "music":

> At first writing was as difficult as reading, and perhaps more so. The patient had forgotten how to hold a pen or to form letters. He was completely helpless. . . . But a discovery he made one day proved to be the turning point: writing could be very simple. At first he had proceeded just as little children do when they first learn to write—he had tried to visualize each letter in order to form it. Yet he had been writing for almost twenty years and as such did not need to employ the same methods as a child, to think about each letter and consider what strokes to use. For adults, writing is an automatic skill, a series of built-in movements which I call "kinetic melodies." Hence, why shouldn't he try to use what skills he still had? . . . In this way he started to write. He no longer

had to agonize over each letter, trying to remember how it was formed. *He could write spontaneously, without thinking.*

Spontaneously! Spontaneously, yes that was the answer. Something spontaneous must happen—or nothing would happen at all.

CHAPTER FIVE

SOLVITUR AMBULANDO

Every disease is a musical problem, every cure a musical solution.

—Novalis

I stood up—or, rather, I was stood up, hoisted to my feet, by two stout physiotherapists—helping as best as I could with the two stout crutches I had been given. I found this bizarre and terrifying. When I looked straight ahead, I had no idea where my left leg was, nor indeed any definite feeling of its existence. I had to look down, for vision was crucial. And when I did look down I had momentary difficulty in recognizing the "object" next to my right foot as my left foot. It did not seem to "belong" to me in any way. I never thought of putting any weight on it, of using it at all. So I stood, or was stood, supported not by my legs, but by crutches and physiotherapists, in a strange, and rather terrifying, stillness—that intense stillness which occurs when something momentous is about to happen.

Into this stillness, this transfixion, brisk voices broke in.

"Come on, Dr. Sacks! You can't stand there like that —like a stork on one leg. You've got to use the other one, put weight on it too!"

"What 'other one'," I was tempted to ask, thinking, How *could* I walk, how *could* I stand on, let alone move, a ghostly lump of jelly, a nothing, which hung loosely from my hip? And even if, supported by its carapace of chalk, this preposterous appendage *could* support me, how then would I "walk" when I had forgotten how to walk?

"Come on, Dr. Sacks!" the physiotherapists urged. "You've got to begin."

To begin! How could I? And yet I must. This was the moment, the singularity, from which beginning must begin.

I could not bring myself to put weight directly on the left leg—because this was strictly an unthinkable, as well as a fearful, thing to do. What I could do, and did do, was to lift the right leg, so that the left leg (so-called) would have to bear weight, or collapse.

Suddenly, with no warning, no anticipation whatever, I found myself precipitated into a vertigo of apparitions. The floor seemed miles away, and then a few inches; the room suddenly tilted and turned on its axis. An acute shock of bewilderment and terror seized me. I felt myself falling, and exclaimed to the therapists:

"Hold me, you must hold me—I'm utterly helpless."

They said, "Now steady yourself—keep your eyes up."

But I was infinitely unsteady, and had to gaze down. There and then I perceived the source of commotion. The source was my leg—or, rather, that thing, that featureless cylinder of chalk which served as my leg—that chalky-white abstraction of a leg. Now the cylinder was a thousand feet long, now a matter of two millimeters; now it was fat, now it was thin; now it was tilted this way, now tilted that. It was constantly changing in size and shape, in position and angle, the changes occurring four or five times a second. The extent of transformation and change was immense—there could be a thousandfold switch between successive "frames." . . .

While the changes were so monstrous in extent and surprise, it was out of the question for me to do anything without being held. It was impossible to proceed with such an instability of image, every parameter unpredictably varying by many orders of magnitude. Within a minute or two (that is to say, after several hundred transformations) the changes became less wild and erratic, although continuing at the same rate as before: the conformations and transformations of the chalk cylinder, though still outrageous, were being modulated and damped, beginning to approach acceptable limits.

At this juncture, then, I decided to move. Besides, I was being urged, even physically levered and pushed, by the two physiotherapists, who perceived my consternation and showed some sympathy, but who nevertheless (I surmised, and later ascertained) had not the faintest idea of the sort of experience I was going through, or contending with, at this time. It was just conceivable (I now thought) that one might learn to operate such a leg—although it would be like operating an extraordinarily unstable robotic contraption, constantly varying in an inherently improbable and unpredictable way. Could one, indeed, make a single successful step, in a world, a perceptual world, constantly altering in shape and size?

As soon as the tumult of sensations and apparitions burst forth, I had the sense of an explosion, of an absolute wildness and chaos, something utterly random and anarchic at work. But *what* could produce such an explosion in my mind? Could it be a mere sensory explosion from the leg, as it was forced to bear weight, and stand, and function, for the first time? Surely the perceptions were too complex for this. They had the quality of constructs, and not of "raw sensations," "sense-data," etc. They had the quality of hypotheses, of space itself, of those elemental *a priori* intuitions without which no perception, or construction of the world, would be possible. The chaos was not of perception itself, but of space, or measure, which precedes perception. I felt that I was bearing witness, even as I was undergoing it, to the very foundations of measure, of mensuration, of a world.

And this perception, or pre-perception or intuition, had nothing whatever to do with me—it was proceeding in its own extraordinary and implacable way; which started, and remained, essentially random, while being modulated by some sort of matching or testing, a targeting or guessing, perhaps a trial-and-error process, a wonderful yet somewhat mechanical sort of computation. I was present, it is true, but only as an observer—a mere spectator at a primordial event, or "Big Bang," which was the start of inner space, the microcosm, in me. I was not actively, but passively, undergoing these changes, and as such could bear witness to what it was like to be present at the founding of a world. A true miracle was being enacted before me, within me. Out of nothingness, out of chaos, measure was being made. The jumping fluttering metrics were converging towards some average—a proto-scale. I felt terror, but also awe and exhilaration of spirit. Within me there seemed to be the working of a cosmic mathematics, the establishment of an impersonal microcosmic order.

All at once I thought of God's questions to Job: "Where wast thou when I laid the foundations of the earth? Who hath laid the measures thereof?" And I thought, with awe, I am there, I have seen it. The frames, the fluttering frames, made me think of Planck and Einstein, and how quantality and relativity may stem from one birth. I felt I was experiencing the "pre-Planck time" of myself—that unimaginable time cosmologists speak of—in the first 10^{-45} seconds after the "Big Bang"—when space is still unstable, fluttering, quantal: that time of preparation which precedes the beginning of real time.

I stood still, arrested, riveted to the spot, partly because the vertigo made movement impossible, partly perhaps because I was arrested by these reflections. My soul was transfixed in a rapture of wonder. "This is the most wonderful thing I have ever known," I thought. "Never must I forget this marvelous moment. Nor can I possibly keep this to myself." And following straight on this thought came more words out of Job: "Oh, that my words were now written! Oh, that they were printed in a book!" In that moment I knew I must describe my experiences.

Never have I so known the swiftness of thought: never have I so known the swiftness of perception. All this which takes so long to relate—thinking of sensation being re-kindled in the leg, and in higher, unused co-ordinating systems; of these, at first so wild and chaotic, being calibrated and corrected by some trial-and-error method; of my mind as a torrent of different perceptions, and perceptual hypotheses and computations, succeeding one another with inconceivable rapidity—passed through my mind in a flash.

I must have presented a strange sight to the good therapists, who probably saw an obviously unstable, staggering, confounded man, with a look at first of consternation on his face, gradually regaining his equilibrium; at first perplexed and fearful, then fascinated and intent, and finally joyful and at peace.

"You went through some changes there, Dr. Sacks," said one of them. "How about taking the first step now?"

The first step! In my efforts to stand, to gain control, I had thought only of holding-on, of survival, or standing, and not yet of moving. Now, I thought, I might try to move. And I was being urged, perhaps even gently pushed and levered, by the therapists, who knew one thing for certain: that one must "get on with it," one must proceed, one must take the first step. They knew—priceless knowledge, which the mind can forget—that there is no substitute, ever, for *doing*, that "In the beginning is the deed," and that there is no path to doing, no way of doing, other than doing.

My first step! Easier said than done.

"Well, Dr. Sacks, what are we waiting for?"

"I can't move," I replied. "I can't think how to. I have no idea whatever how to take the first step."

"Why?" she said. "You were able to make a flexion-movement at the hip yesterday. You were so excited about it—and now you can't take a step!"

"It is one thing to flex the leg in bed," I replied, "but quite another to take the first step."

She gave me a long look and then, seeing the useless-
ness of words, wordlessly moved my left leg with her leg,
pushing it to a new position, so that it made, or was made
to make, a sort of step. Once this was done, I saw how to
do it. I could not be told, but could instantly be shown—
and she showed me what such a movement was like, as
the at first involuntary, or tic-like, flexion the day before
had shown me what hip-flexion was like, so that, having
been shown, I could bring my will to bear, and do it
actively for myself. Once the first step was made, even
though it was an artificial, not a spontaneous, "step," I saw
how to do it—how I might flex the hip in such a way that
the leg moved forwards a reasonable distance.

In order to judge what was a "reasonable distance," in
a "reasonable direction," I found myself entirely dependent
on external, or visual, landmarks—marks on the floor, or
marks triangulated with reference to the furniture and
walls. I had to work out each step fully, and in advance,
and then advance the leg, cautiously, empirically, until it
had reached the point I had calculated and designated as
secure.

Why did I "walk" in this ludicrous fashion? Because,
I found, I had no choice. For if I didn't look down, and let
the leg "move by itself," it was liable to move four inches
or four feet, and also to move in the wrong direction—for
example, sideways, or, most commonly, at randomly slant-
ing angles. On several occasions, indeed, before I realized I
would have to "program" its movements in advance and
monitor them constantly, it "got lost," and almost tripped
me up, by somehow getting stuck behind, or otherwise entangled with, my normal right leg.

The unreality was still extreme. It wasn't "my" leg I

was walking with, but a huge, clumsy prosthesis (or hypothesis), a bizarre appendage, a leg-shaped cylinder of chalk—a cylinder, moreover, which was still constantly altering, fluttering, in shape and size, as if I was operating a peculiarly clumsy, and unstable, robotic contraption, an absolutely ludicrous artificial leg. I cannot convey, except in this way, how strange this pseudo-walking was—how entirely lacking in any sense, and, conversely, how over-loaded with a painstaking mechanical exactitude and caution. I found it a matter of the most elaborate and ex-hausting and tedious computation. It was locomotion of a sort, but unanimal, unhuman. "This is walking?" I said to myself, and then, with a qualm of terror: "Is this what I will have to put up with for the rest of my life? Will I never get back the *feel* of true walking? Will I never again know a walking which is natural, spontaneous, and free? Will I be forced, from now on, to think out each move? Must every-thing be so complex—can't it be simple?"

And suddenly—into the silence, the silent twittering of motionless frozen images—came music, glorious music, Mendelssohn, *fortissimo*! Joy, life, intoxicating movement! And, as suddenly, without thinking, without intending whatever, I found myself walking, easily-joyfully, *with* the music. And, as suddenly, in the moment that this inner music started, the Mendelssohn which had been summoned and hallucinated by my soul, and in the very moment that my "motor" music, my kinetic melody, my walking, came back—in this self-same moment *the leg came back*. Sud-denly, with no warning, no transition whatever, the leg felt alive, and real, and mine, its moment of actualization pre-cisely consonant with the spontaneous quickening, walking and music. I was just turning back from the corridor to my room—when out of the blue this miracle occurred—the music, the walking, the actualization, all one. And now, as suddenly, I was absolutely certain—I *believed* in my leg, I *knew* how to walk . . .

I said to the physiotherapists: "Something extraordinary has just occurred. I can walk now. Let me go—but you had better stand by!"

And walk I did—despite weakness, despite the cast, despite crutches, despite everything—easily, automatically, spontaneously, melodiously, with a return of my own personal melody, which was somehow elicited by, and attuned to, the Mendelssohnian melody.

I walked with style—with a style which was inimitably my own. Those who saw this echoed my own feelings. They said: "You walked mechanically, like a robot before—now you walk like a person—like yourself, in fact."

It was as if I suddenly remembered how to walk—indeed, not "as if." *I remembered how to walk*. All of a sudden I remembered walking's natural, unconscious rhythm and melody; it came to me, suddenly, like remembering a once-familiar but long-forgotten tune, and it came hand-in-hand with the Mendelssohn rhythm and tune. There was an abrupt and absolute leap at this moment—not a process, not a transition, but a transilience,—from the awkward, artificial, mechanical walking, of which every step had to be consciously counted, projected, and undertaken—to an unconscious, natural-graceful, musical movement.

Again I thought instantly of Zazetsky, in *The Man with a Shattered World*, and *his* "turning-point," as recounted by Luria—the sudden discovery he made one day, that writing, previously desperately difficult, as he agonized over each letter and stroke, could become perfectly simple if he let himself go, if he gave himself, unconsciously and unreservedly, to its natural flow, melody, spontaneity. And then I thought of countless, though less spectacular, experiences of my own—times when I had set out to run or swim, first counting and calculating each step or stroke consciously, and then, quite suddenly, discovering that I had got "into it," that I had, mysteriously, without in the least trying, got "into the hang," "into the rhythm," "into the feel," of the activity, and that now I was doing it perfectly and easily, with no conscious counting or calculation whatever, but simply giving myself to the activity's own tempo, pulsion and rhythm. The experience was so common I had hardly given it a thought, but now, I suddenly realized, the experience was fundamental.

Had I had any thought that the coincidence of ambulation and actualization with the Mendelssohn was a freak —a mere coincidence, of no special significance—the idea was to be dissipated forty seconds later, when, striding along, full of confidence, I had a sudden and unexpected relapse—suddenly forgot my kinetic melody, forgot how to walk. In this moment, as suddenly as if the needle had been lifted from a record, the inner playing of the Mendelssohn stopped, and in the instant it stopped my walking stopped too. Suddenly the leg ceased to be stable and real and reverted to its cinematic delirium, its awful wild jumping of shapes, sizes, frames. As soon as the music stopped the walking stopped too and the leg was de-actualized into fluttering phantoms. How could I doubt the significance of all this? The music, the action, the reality were all one.

I was helpless, once again, and could hardly stand.

The two physiotherapists guided me to a rail, which I grabbed and held onto with all my strength.

The left leg flopped nervelessly. I touched it, and it was toneless, unreal.

"Don't worry," said one of them. "It's local fatigue. Give the nerve terminals a little rest, and it'll come right again."

Half-propped against the rail, half-standing on my good leg, I rested the left leg. The delirium diminished, the excursions grew less wild, though fluttering at the same rate. After two minutes or so, there was sufficient stability. With my supporters, I ventured forth again. And now, for the second time, the music came back, as suddenly as at first, and with its return there came back spontaneous, joyous, thoughtless walking, and tone and actuality to the leg. Luckily it was only a few yards to my room and I was able to retain the music, and musicality, of motion, until I had gained my chair and, from this, my bed, exhausted but triumphant.

In bed I was ecstatic. A miracle seemed to have happened. The reality of my leg, and the power to stand and walk again, had been given to me, had descended upon me like grace. Now, re-united with my leg—with a part of myself that had been excommunicated, in Limbo—I found myself full of tender regard for it, and stroked the cast. I felt an immense feeling of Welcome for the lost leg, now returned. The leg had come home, to its home, to me. In action the body had been broken, and only now, with the return of bodily action as a whole, did the body itself again feel like a whole.

Until the music, there had been no feeling whatever—

that is, no essential feeling in the phenomena themselves. This was especially clear in the fantastic few minutes of kaleidoscopic, flashing vision. It was spectacular, the most spectacular display I had ever seen in my life; but it was only a spectacle, and I only a spectator. There was no "entering," nor any thought or possibility of entering, these purely sensorial and intellectual phenomena. One gazed at them as one would gaze at fireworks, or the sky. They could be seen as having a cold and impersonal beauty, the beauty of mathematics, of astronomy, the sky.

Then, all of a sudden, with no warning whatever, into the cold starry impersonal cosmos—the equally cold and impersonal micro-cosmos of the mind—came *music*, warm, vivid, alive, moving, personal. Music, as I had dreamed at the weekend, was a divine message and messenger of life. It was quintessentially quick—"the quickening art," as Kant had called it—quickening my soul, and with this my body, so that suddenly, spontaneously, I was quickened into motion, my own perceptual and kinetic melody, quickened into life by the inner life of music. And in that moment, when the body became action, the leg, the flesh became quick and alive, the flesh became music, incarnate solid music. All of me, body and soul, became music in that moment:

> You are the music
> while the music lasts.
> —Eliot

Everything was transformed, absolutely, in that moment, in that leap from a cold fluttering and flashing to the warm stream of music, the stream of action, the stream of life.

The delirium, the pandemonium, the kaleidoscope, the cinema—this was essentially inanimate, discontinuous; whereas the stream of music, of action, of life, was essentially, and entirely, and indivisibly, a stream, an organic whole, without any separations or seams, but articulate, articulated, articulate with life. An entirely new principle came into effect—what Leibniz called a "new *active* principle of unity"—a unity only present in, and given by, action.

What was so wonderful was the heavenly ease and sureness—I knew what to do, I knew what came next, I was carried ahead by the ongoing musical stream, without any conscious thought or calculation, carried ahead by the feeling of it all. And it was this that was so different, so absolutely different, from the elaborate and exhausting computation before—the sense that everything had to be counted and worked out beforehand, to be worked out as programs, strategies, procedures, and that nothing could be simply, thoughtlessly, *done*. The joy of sheer doing—its beauty, its simplicity—was a revelation: it was the easiest, most natural thing in the world—and yet beyond the most complex of calculations and programs. Here, in doing, one achieved certainty with one swoop, by a grace which bypassed the most complex mathematics, or perhaps embedded and then transcended them. Now, simply, everything felt right, everything *was* right, with no effort, but with an integral sense of ease—and delight.

What was it, then, that came suddenly back—embodied in music, glorious music, Mendelssohn, *fortissimo*? It was the triumphal return of the quintessential living "I," lost for two weeks in the abyss, and two minutes in the delirium; not the ghostly, cogitating, solipsistic "I" of

Descartes, which never feels, never acts, *is* not, and *does* nothing; not this, this impotence, this mentalistic fiction. What came, what announced itself, so palpably, so gloriously, was a full-bodied vital feeling and action, originating from an aboriginal, commanding, willing, "I." The phantasmagoria, the delirium, had no organization, no center. What appeared with the music was organization and center, and the organization and center of all action was an agency, an "I." What appeared in this moment transcended the physical, but instantly organized and re-organized it into a seamless perfect Whole. This new, hyper-physical principle was Grace. Grace, unbidden, appeared on the scene, became its center, transformed the scene. Grace entered, as Grace enters, at the very center of things, at its hidden innermost inaccessible center, and instantly coordinated, subordinated, all phenomena to itself. It made the next move obvious, certain, natural. Grace was the prerequisite and essence of all *doing*.

Solvitur ambulando: the solution to the problem of walking is—walking. The only way to do it is—to do it. The key to this paradox is the mystery of Grace. Here action and thought reached their end and repose. I had had the most eventful and crucial ten minutes of my life.

CHAPTER SIX

CONVALESCENCE

Gratitude pours forth continually, as if the unexpected had just happened—the gratitude of a convalescent—for *convalescence* was unexpected . . . [One] is now all at once attacked by hope, . . . the *intoxication* of convalescence . . . after long privation and powerlessness, the rejoicing of a strength that is returning, of a reawakened faith in a tomorrow and the day after tomorrow, of a sudden sense and anticipation of a future, of impending adventures, of seas that are open again, of goals that are permitted again, believed again.

—Nietzsche

Freedom! Now, suddenly, I could walk, I was free. Now, suddenly, I was whole, I was well. At least I could feel what wholeness, wellness, felt like, where they had been unimaginable—beyond thought, beyond hope—before. Now, suddenly, walking, I knew again a physical or animal freedom—prelude, perhaps, to any other freedom. Now, suddenly, vistas opened up—where, hardly realizing it, I had seen nothing before. I had lain or sat, virtually motion-less, as if paralyzed, for eighteen days in my room, eighteen days of intense thought, but without *doing* or *going*. I was not free, physically free, to do or go. But now I could, as by a miracle, stand; and simply by standing, being able to stand, my "standing," in all respects, was radically changed.

In the moments of first standing and walking—or, more accurately, the moment that immediately followed—I found I felt completely different: no longer prostrate, passive-dependent, like a patient, but active, erect, able to face a new world—a real world, *a world now made possible*, instead of the shifting half-world of patienthood and confinement I had been in. I could stand up, step forward, go from and to—from confinement and patient-hood to a real world, a real self, whose very existence, incredibly, and ominously, I had half forgotten. Yes, stewing in confinement, passivity, immobility: stewing in the depths of *scotoma* and despair; stewing in the darkness of interminable night, I had forgotten, could no longer imagine, what daylight felt like.

Back in my room, on my bed, I hugged the redeemed leg, or rather cast, though even this seemed living now, transfused with the life of the leg. "You dear old thing, you sweet thing," I found myself saying. "You've come back, you're real, you're part of me now." Its reality, its presence, its dearness, were all one. I gazed at it in a sort of bliss, filled with the sense of intense physicality, but a physicality radiant and almost supernatural—no longer an uncanny, ghastly-ghostly dough, but "the holy and glorious flesh" restored. I felt aflame with amazement, gratitude, joy—aflame with love, worship, praise. "Thank

God," I cried, and "God be praised"—ejaculations, verbal forms, which suddenly had sense.

I had tried and tried for at least fourteen days, to *think* the leg back into life and reality—utterly useless efforts, as vain as they were strenuous. And now, without thinking, without trying, the leg was there—wondrously, unassailably, gloriously there. It seemed radiant in its over-whelming and immediate *thereness*—that thereness now given, which no thinking could reach. (Not passively, but actively there—its thereness, its presence, being one with potential: a thing of power now, bodied power, which I could move as I wished.)

For 300 hours, motionless, in my room, on my bed, I had lain still, and thought. One "stops to think," one is arrested by thought; and being stopped, being arrested, in my senses and body, removed from doing, I was forced into thinking. Now the time for thinking was over, and the time for doing had come; now—and for the weeks ahead—my flight would be swift, intuitive, unreflective; I would return to my body, my being, the world, to the special adventure of convalescence and rebirth; I was to come alive again, and *know* life, as never before.

On the succeeding days my walking was much better. It came daily more easily, more fluently, more musically, although with fatigue I would fall back into "delirium"—flashing images without inner sense or motion. But with each walk, and each day, I found myself stronger, and able to walk further before delirium set in. It occurred, for the last time, about a month after surgery, after I had walked for miles in the great grounds of the Convalescent Home in Kenwood. I have never known the experience since.

With each succeeding day, each success, I grew bolder —overbold—and had to be held back from "overdoing" it, pushing the leg, if not to delirium, to swelling and strain. The return of health and strength—convalescence—was intoxicating, and I continually misjudged what I could or should do; and yet it wasn't smooth, it consisted of steps— with no spontaneous advancement from one stage, or one step, to another. When I stole a look at my chart and saw "Uneventful Recovery," I thought: "They're mad. Recovery *is* events, a series of wonderful, unpredictable events: recovery is events, or rather advents—the advent of new and unimaginable powers—events, advents, which are births or re-births."

Recovery was not to be seen as a smooth slope, but as a series of radical steps, each inconceivable, impossible, from the step below. And, by the same token, one could have not even hope. One could hope for an increase of whatever one had, but one could not hope, in the least, for the unimaginable next step (for hope implies some degree of imagining). Thus every step had the quality of miracle —and might never occur without the urging of others.

With each step, each advance, one's horizons expanded, one stepped out of a contracted world—a world one hadn't realized was so contracted. I found this in every sphere, physiological and existential. One example comes specially to mind: three days after my first walk, I was moved into a new room, a new spacious room, after twenty days in my tiny cell. I was settling myself, with delight, when I suddenly noticed something most strange. Everything close to me had its proper solidity, spaciousness, depth—but everything farther away was totally flat. Beyond my open door was the door of the ward opposite;

beyond this a patient seated in a wheelchair; beyond him, on the windowsill, a vase of flowers; and beyond this, over the road, the gabled windows of the house opposite—and all this, two hundred feet perhaps, was flat as a pancake, and seemed to lie like a giant Kodachrome in the air, exquisitely colored and detailed, but perfectly flat. I have very good depth perception and I suddenly realized that something had happened to my sense of depth and stereoscopy, that it stopped, quite suddenly, a few feet in front of me—that I was still enclosed, visually, in a transparent box, about nine by seven by six feet, the precise size of the "cell" I had occupied for twenty days. I was still *in* this, perceptually, despite being moved—still *in* a grossly restricted visual space with perfect stereoscopy to its limits, and no trace of it beyond. It was a bizarre experience, which fascinated (without frightening) me—for it was not charged, like the leg, with terrible trauma and fear. I could observe, even measure, the parallactic displacements which are normally seen as "depth," but noting this, knowing this, did not restore depth. Depth, stereoscopy, returned in jumps, like the jerky opening-out of a visual concertina, over a period of about two hours; and even then it was not complete, for turning over in bed and gazing out of the window—bliss! I had been windowless, vistaless, for twenty days—I could see, as though through the wrong end of a telescope, the tiny gem-like hospital garden, but absolutely flat, and with its angles all wrong, looking distorted, trapezoidal, when it was, obviously, a square. And I had now to gaze at this, beyond my previous far-point, until *its* distance and depth and appearance jumped right.

I was amazed and fascinated by these visual experiences, which appeared to me, in some sense, analogous to the leg. Stereoscopy, so it seemed, had partly disappeared, to precisely the extent of my visual deprivation—just as the leg had disappeared, totally, with total sensory and motor deprivation. I could be fascinated by the visual changes, without any fear. And yet, despite this, despite other differences, there seemed to be a curious analogy: deprivation, non-use, in both cases, had been at work—with spectacular, bizarre (and, in the leg's case, quite dreadful) consequences. There was nothing dreadful about the loss of stereoscopy, but it was still, nevertheless, quite drastic and radical. I had never realized that stereoscopy *could* be confined. I wondered what happened to prisoners confined in small cells. And I immediately bought a stereoscope and donated it to the ward, with the thought that it might be used by future patients, confined in small spaces, to protect them against "prisoner syndrome"—the resultant contractions of visual space.

Room, space, expansion. Freedom—an ever-expanding physiology and world, an ever-expanding personal (and social) space—this, it came to me, with extreme clarity, this was the essence of getting-better, convalescence—not merely in the specific realm of my leg and mobility, not merely in the technical realm of stereoscopy and visuality, but in the whole general realm of coming to life, emerging from self-absorption, sickness, patienthood, and confinement, to the spaciousness of health, of full being, of the real world—which, rather terrifyingly, I had largely forgotten, in the short space of three weeks as a patient.

Not the least part of the terror was that I experienced no terror. I had no sense, no realization, of how contracted I was, how insensibly I had become contracted to the locus of my sickbed and sickroom—contracted in the most literal, physiological terms, but contracted too in imagination and feeling. I had become a pygmy, a prisoner, an inmate—a patient—without the faintest awareness. We speak, glibly, of "institutionalization," without the smallest personal sense of what is involved—how insidious, and universal, is the contraction in all realms (not least the moral realm), and how swiftly it can happen to anyone, oneself.

I had often spoken to my own patients, institutionalized for decades before their "awakening," and asked them —Did they not feel terribly confined? Did they not yearn for the great world outside? And I would be amazed and incredulous when they quietly said "No." I could not see them all as pathological—and yet this complaisance seemed almost universal, and retarded and obstructed their return to spaciousness and fullness of life, even when this had been rendered physically possible by L-DOPA. Now, I realized, such regression was universal. It would occur with any immobilization, illness, or confinement. It was an unavoidable, natural shrinking-down of existence, made both bearable and untreatable because not realizable—not directly realizable. How could one know that one had shrunk, if one's frame of reference had itself shrunk? One had to be reminded of the great world one had "forgotten" —and then, only then, could one expand and be cured.

That same happy Saturday—the day I was moved from my windowless, tiny, solitary cell to a spacious room on the orthopedic ward, the day when *visual* space and spaciousness was restored to me, a day on which I walked half a mile, which gave me a great sense of *motor* strength and space—that same happy Saturday (just three weeks after my fall—the longest and shortest, fullest and emptiest, three weeks of my life) saw a *moral* liberation, too.

There had been, for me—and perhaps there must be for all patients, for it is a condition of patienthood (though, one hopes, one which can be well- and not ill-handled)—two miseries, two afflictions, conjoined, yet distinct. One was the physical (and "physical-existential") disability—the organically determined erosion of being and space. The other was "moral"—not quite an adequate word—associated with the reduced stationless status of a patient, and, in particular, conflict with and surrender to "them"—"them" being the surgeon, the whole system, the institution—a conflict with hateful and even paranoid tones, which added to the severe, yet neutral, physical affliction a far less tolerable, because irresoluble, moral affliction. I had felt not only physically but morally prostrate—unable to stand up, stand morally before "them," in particular, before the surgeon. And though I knew, at some level, all the time, that he was a decent man, and so was I, and that everyone meant well and was doing his best, yet I couldn't shake off the nightmare feeling which had lain on me, doubtless to some extent since admission, but which became acute and specific when communications broke down—when the surgeon said, with authority, that there was "nothing," and so contradicted and questioned and doubted my (most elemental) perceptions—perceptions on which my most elemental sense of "I," self-integrity, was based. When I felt physically helpless, immobile, confined, I felt morally helpless, paralyzed, contracted, confined—and not just contracted, but contorted as well, into roles and postures of abjection.

On Saturday, then, I called on the surgeon. Previously

I had passively awaited *his* calls, which were always in the odious context of "rounds," where before a massive team he had to play the role of all-wise consultant and I the role of all-passive patient. I called on the surgeon, and had "a good talk"—a wise talk, a human talk, which took us both off the hook.

Such a talk was possible, now, because I needed him less. I no longer felt critically (and resentfully) dependent. It was possible because my world had enlarged—and so he, the system, the institution, could shrink, shrink into a reasonable and proper perspective. And clearly for him this was a relief too, because nobody wants a vexatious, vexed patient, nor did he want to play ogre in my dream. Peace was established, with propriety, dignity—and some hint of an amused, but reserved, cordiality.

Now I was free—morally free, as well as physically free—to make the long trek, the return, which still lay before me. Now the moral obscurity and darkness was lifted, as well as the physical darkness, the shadow, the *scotoma*. Now the road lay open before me into the land of light and life. Now, unimpeded, without conflict or blocks, I would run this good road, swifter and swifter, into a joy, a fullness and sweetness of life, such as I had forgotten, or never known. My spirits had been rising since that wonder-walk on Wednesday, and now, on Saturday, I was flying with joy—a joy which was to last, and deepen, for six weeks, which transformed, and transfigured the world, and made of everything a new wonder and festivity.

A peculiar delight suffused the garden outside my window. There had been no real outside before, no daylight, no sun rising and setting, no grass, no trees, no sense of space or life. Like a man parched, I gazed thirstily, yearningly, at the green quadrangle, only realizing how cut off from life I had been, in my sterile, windowless, artificial cubicle. No picture sufficed. I had to see—and since it was still physically very difficult for me, at least for the hours I still spent in bed, I gazed at its reflection in my shaving mirror held aloft. And through the mirror, tiny but real, I saw figures in the garden, sitting and strolling— my first glimpse of the real world, the human world, outside. Visually, in tiny reflection, I hugged this to myself, and longed above all to go down to this garden (though it didn't occur to me that this would ever actually be possible: it still seemed, in some way, unattainable, or forbidden). Every step, every advance, needed a kind of "permission." This feeling of being shut-up and kept-in was extraordinarily intense, the more so for being, for the most part, unconscious and unrealized. Moreover it was often I myself who prohibited, or inhibited, free speech and action—that part of myself which was now the institution internalized. And now, for the first time finding myself with other patients, I would see this in them where I failed to see it in myself; and I would see that something or someone was needed to break the barrier of prohibition or inhibition—whether is was someone "giving permission," or the sudden insight that no "permission" was required. This too made recovery step-wise. There was, so to speak, a ladder of freedom to be climbed rung by rung, the ascent of which needed a double prerequisite—the necessary degree of organic recovery and the necessary audacity, permission, or moral freedom.

"Uneventful recovery." What damned utter nonsense! Recovery (as the good Registrar said) was a "pilgrimage," a journey, in which one moved, if one moved, stage by stage, or by stations. Every stage, every station, was a completely new advent, requiring a new start, a new birth or beginning. One had to begin, to be born, again and again. Recovery was an exercise in nothing short of birth, for as mortal man grows sick, and dies, by stages, so natal man grows well, and is quickened, by stages—radical stages, existence-stages, absolute and new: unexpected, unexpectable, incalculable and surprising. Recovery uneventful? It *consists* of events!

After Saturday events moved quicker—or in broad, historical sweeps. I ceased to keep a minute diary or journal, and, to some extent, ceased "observation" and recording altogether, being carried along in the broad sweep, the spate, of recovery. And, as importantly, I was no longer alone, but one of many, a ward, a community, of patients. I was no longer the only one in the world, as perhaps every patient thinks in the ultimate solitude of illness. I was no longer confined to my own, empty world, but found myself in a world peopled by others—*real* others, at least in relation to each other and me: not just role-players, good or bad, as my caretakers had been. Only now could I exorcise the fearful words of the surgeon to me: "You're unique!" Now, speaking freely to my fellow patients—a freedom made possible precisely by fellowship, by the fact that they were, *we* were, brothers together, under no status pressure to conceal or distort—now enjoying free commerce, for the first time, I learned that my own experience, my "case," was far from unique. Almost every patient who had had injury or surgery to a limb, and whose limb had then been casted, out of sight, out of action, had experienced, at least, some degree of alienation: I heard of hands and feet which felt "queer," "wrong," "strange," "unreal," "uncanny," "detached," and "cut off—and, again, and again, the phrase "like nothing on earth." I was on the ward six days, and spoke fully and freely to all patients there. Many, it was apparent, had had experiences like mine; and none, it was clear, had communicated this successfully to the surgeon. Some had tried, and been rebuffed, like me; most had preserved a reticent silence; none had actually managed to get through. Some had been terrified, others mildly scared; a few, stolid or stoic, seemed indifferent, saying, "Nah, I didn't worry. It's just one of those things." If, indeed, I was "unique," it was not in regard to the experience or its character, but only in the reflection, the ceaseless thought, I brought to it—the sense of "reason's violation," and its fundamental importance.

As soon as I had ascertained this, the investigator in me rested, and I could slip into a more normal, social relation. But all of us were still somewhat solitary and isolated at this stage—from the essential aloneness and privacy of illness, and the isolation enforced by the rigid "vertical" structure of the institution.

My six days on the ward were social to a point—but to a necessarily limited point. It was only later, in the Convalescent Home, that the "atmosphere" changed, that isolation and "institutionalization" fell away, like a bad dream, and gave way to a delightful cozy-homey atmosphere with a sense, often intense, of fellowship and friendship, and of an essentially communal and convivial life, living together, getting well together—the essential sharing and "con" of convalescence.

The day before my transfer to Kenwood, the Convalescent Home in Hampstead, I was taken down to the little garden I had so yearningly gazed at—taken down in a wheelchair, dressed in hospital pajamas. This was a great joy—to be out in the air—for I had not been outside in almost a month. A pure and intense joy, a blessing, to feel the sun on my face and the wind in my hair, to hear birds, to see, touch and fondle the living plants. Some essential connection and communion with nature was re-established after the horrible isolation and alienation I had known. Some part of me came alive, when I was taken to the garden, which had been starved, and died, perhaps without my knowing it. I suddenly felt what I have often felt intensely before, but never thought to apply to my own time in hospital: that one needs open-air hospitals with gardens, set in country and woods—like some of the Little Sisters' Homes I work in in rural New York; a hospital like a home, not a fortress or "institution"; a hospital like a home —and perhaps like a village.

But if I rejoiced in the blessing of the sun, I found I was avoided by the non-patients in the gardens—the students, nurses, visitors who came there. I was set apart, we were set apart, we patients in white nightgowns, and avoided clearly, though unconsciously, like lepers. Nothing gave me such a sense of the social caste of patients, their being out-cast, outcasts, set apart by society: the pity, the abhorrence, our white gowns inspired—the sense of a complete gulf between us and them, which courtesy and ceremony served only to emphasize. I realized how I myself, in health, in the past, had shuddered away from patients, quite unconsciously, never realizing it for a moment. But now, sick myself, garbed and gowned as a patient, I was intensely conscious of how I was shuddered-from, how the healthy, the non-patients, kept a distance between us. Had I not been so fearful and self-involved on admission, I might have seen more clearly what "admission" involved —the hospital clothes, the name-tag, the removal of individuality, the reduction to a generic status and identity; but, curiously, it took that scene in the garden to show me, diagrammatically, and almost comically, how set-apart we were—and the gulf which would have to be bridged or leapt before one could fully rejoin the world of men.

The gap, the abyss, between sickness and health—this was what the Convalescent Home was for—we had become invalids, in-valid. We had resided in sickness too long. And we had not only harbored it, but become sick ourselves—developed the attitudes of inmates and invalids. Now we needed a double recovery—a physical recovery, and a spiritual movement *to* health. It was not enough to be physically well, if we still felt the fear and the care of the ill. We had all, in our ways, been undermined by sickness—had lost the careless boldness, the freedom, of the well. We could not be thrown back into the world straightaway. We had to have an in-between—existential as well as medical, a place where we could live a limited existence —limited and protected, not too demanding—a limited, but steadily enlarging, existence—until we were ready to re-enter the great world. The acute hospital was scarcely a world at all, as acute injury or illness was scarcely a life. Now we were improved, and needed world and life, but could not face, would be destroyed by, the full demands of life, and the bustling, callous, careless hugeness of the world; we needed a quiet place, a haven, a shelter, where we could gradually regain our confidence and health, our confidence no less than our health—a peaceful interlude, a Sabbath-world, something like college, where we could grow morally and physically strong.

It also struck me, this last day in hospital, that convalescence, and special places for it, was a social no less than an individual need. If we, freshly sick, could not face the world, the world could not face us, with our lineaments, our habiliments, of sickness and affliction. We inspired horror and fear—I saw this quite clearly—and for the world's sake, no less than our own, could not be let out. We had been stamped, with the stigmata of patients, the intolerable knowledge of affliction and death, the intolerable knowledge of passivity, lost nerve, and dependence— and the world does not care to be reminded of such things. Goffman has talked well of "total institutions"—asylums, prisons—for the wholly set apart, those essentially terrible but perhaps necessary constructs, to keep from public sight the sick, the condemned, the stigmatized. But convalescent homes, like colleges, or cloisters, were different. They had a character essentially benevolent and sweet. They were institutions (if this is not a contradiction in terms) devoted to patience and understanding, to the nurture and re-arming of frail bodies and souls—devoted, centrally, to the individual and his care. Such a convalescent home would indeed be a haven and home, an asylum in the best and truest, deepest sense, and infinitely far from the horror of Goffman's "asylums." And yet . . .

And yet there *had* to be ambivalences here, for though as a sick patient, in hospital, one was reduced to moral infancy, this was not a malicious degradation, but a biological and spiritual need of the hurt creature. One *had* to go back, one *had* to regress, for one might indeed be as helpless as a child, whether one liked it, or willed it, or not. In hospital one became again a child with parents (parents who might be good or bad), and this might be felt as "infantilizing" and degrading, or as a sweet and sorely-needed nourishing. Now came the next stage—the need for growing-up. If morally, existentially, one was a child in hospital, in a convalescent home one would be treated differently—more brusquely, less tenderly: as an adolescent, perhaps.

Consciously, of course, I desired to leave, to graduate from the hospital, and start growing up; and yet, on my last night, my unconscious self contrived a near-accident which, had it been successful, would have kept me in hospital. I had gained, in eight days, a good deal of confidence and strength, was able to walk with my crutches a quarter of a mile at a stretch, to transfer, to balance myself, with verve and panache. It seemed to me no more than exuberance and high spirits that I had an impulse, on my last night, to climb to the roof, even though climbing stairs was a skill I had only just achieved, and this involved not just stairs, but a trapdoor and a ladder. What a thrilling adventure, to climb to the roof, and see the lights of London emblazoning the night sky! Thrilling and—with crutches, and a cast, and a half-denervated leg—absolutely crazy, and potentially lethal. Fortunately, I was spotted before going too far, brought down and lectured sharply on my provocativeness and folly. It was only at this point that it broke through to consciousness, and I realized—I had in fact tried to have an accident, because I was dead scared of leaving. I would not mention a purely private bit of neurotic "acting-out," had I not discovered that such acts were rather common among the patients. All of us, to a man, were "eager to leave," eager to get out, and get on to the next step. And yet this involved a relinquishing of care, of the cherished-infant status we were now used to. We wanted, consciously, to be weaned, but unconsciously we feared, and tried to stop it, to prolong our special, pampered status.

Escapade or no, I was shipped out the next morning, along with half a dozen others—*all* of whom, I found, had had last-minute escapades. And I, by God, was the only able-bodied one there; the others had catheters, were pale or short of breath, or just looked ill, a sorry crew struggling, or being lifted, into the bus. And our bus—like a lazar-ship, ghost-ship, death-ship—seemed to weave a damned route, alien and isolated, to Hampstead.

I found myself frightened—we all were, I think—by the blaze and bustle of the world outside, the speed and violence of the traffic, the huge crowds, the noise. The sheer complexity and bustle of the world was terrifying. We all turned away from the windows, aghast, thankful we were not to be thrown into this, yet. Some of us had scoffed at "a Convalescent Home" ("A silly idea, a silly place, I want to get out"), but none of us wanted this after one look at—the Outside. It was a tremendous relief, a liberation, to be no longer "in," but none of us, we realized, were ready to go "out." The sense, the necessity, of an in-between, became clear, and the "silly" place became, to us, dear, necessary, and desired. It was an immense relief as we got out of the bustling central city and up towards the quieter heights of Hampstead. There was a moment of fear, and then an enchantment, when we came to that manorial gate, which was creakily opened and then closed behind us, and as we drove up to, and were deposited at, the old manor house itself—a huge, old, rambling, ivy-twined building, set in grounds so green and vast that all sight and sense of the city was gone and banished. Gratefully, shakily, we tumbled out of the bus. We were greeted by a kind-faced, motherly matron and, our exhaustion appreciated, taken to our rooms. All of us fell immediately into exhausted, relieved sleep.

I awoke—to a scene of pure magic, a low full moon, a harvest moon, flooding the landscape with light, shining on the low wooded hills all around me. It was, I suddenly realized, just one lunar month since the evening I had rowed across Hardanger fjørd, under just such a full moon, the very night before my fall. That enchanted, mysterious, yet sinister evening, when I had heard music on the still water of the fjørd—a dream, an illusion?—no, a reality, but a magical reality, coming from a lakeside church. How enchanted, scarcely breathing, afraid to break the spell, I had moored the boat, and walked softly through the churchyard, past moonlit graves, to the illuminated house of God, filled and swelling with Mozart's great Mass.

Had a month, a whole month, actually passed? While I lay frothing and fretting in hospital, the heavenly motions had continued, majestically indifferent, sublimely above my ego-charged frenzies. An immense calm, a sublime peace, enfolded the scene. The sense of fret and impatience drained out of me, like a poison. I felt I was one with the vast calm all round me. Waking, that evening, I felt peace like a blessing—a Sabbath-grace, descended from the sky.

There was a light September mist blurring the light, softening all outlines, wreathing and protecting us. This too I felt as a sweetness and blessing—appropriate for the calm interim ahead: "Thank you, thank you, thank you, Fog."

Gently, softly (the violence had gone out of me) I

levered myself out of bed, and on to my crutches. It was late, I had slept through supper, the patients were abed. Softly, gently, I descended the great staircase—how right this old manor was for the period I was now in. All was silent, benignly silent, below—the silence of peace, of repose, of a Sabbath. I closed my eyes and murmured a prayer of thanksgiving and praise.

Who cared if there was really any Being to pray to? What mattered was the sense of giving thanks and praise, the feeling of a humble and grateful heart.

Between the last full moon and this, in the space of a single lunar month, I had come near to death, and been saved at the last moment; had had my mangled flesh sewn together and united; had "lost" my leg (for an eternity?) in a limbo of non-feeling; had recovered it, as by a miracle, when recovery seemed impossible. I had had the foundations of my inner world shaken—nay, I had had them utterly destroyed. I had experienced "reason's scandal," and the humiliation of mind. I had fallen into an abyss, with the breaking apart of my tissues, my perceptions, the natural unities of body-soul, body-mind. And I had been lifted from the abyss, reborn, reaffirmed, by powers beyond my understanding and reason. I had been shaken and foundered—but mysteriously saved. And now I had come to this sweet haven, this old manor-house, in Hampstead, where candles glimmered in human lightness and a vast moonlit calm lay on the hills about me. I opened the door —what a freedom was this, for in the hospital there was no liberty to come and go—and stood, for a minute, in the soft air, savoring its fineness and the sweet smell of woods, and seeing in the distance the nightglow of London, city of cities, my mother.

For some reason, in the hospital, I had found it difficult to weep. I was miserable, frequently, but with a hard,
dry-eyed anguish. Now, suddenly, I found the tears coming down. I wept—joy, gratitude?—without knowing why
I did so.

It was not till breakfast that I met my fellow patients
—all of us patients, convalescents, brought together for a
time. A newcomer, low on the totem-pole, I was assigned
to a table in the corner, an object of curiosity, concern and
perhaps some contempt to the veterans. There was an
instant feeling of group—and hierarchy—like a first day
in army or school—but beneath this, a warm and com-
radely feeling.

Straightaway I ran into a problem: I could not bring
my crutches to the table, but if I disposed of them, how
could I *get* to the table?

"See here," said my neighbor, seeing me puzzled and
awkward. "Sit yourself down, and I'll put your crutches
in the corner. We all have to help each other here."

I thanked him. He was a little grizzled man, a dia-
betic, who had just had an amputation and was much
plagued, he confessed, by vivid phantoms. We introduced
ourselves quasi-medically, with our symptoms and problems, and only later in a more personal way.

"What about you? What happened?" he asked, with
a glance at the cast.

I told him.

"Isn't that the darnedest thing!" He turned to the
others. "Doc here's got a leg, but no feeling in the leg—
and I've got the feeling, but no leg to go with it! You
know—" (he turned back to me) "we could make one

good leg between us. I'll donate the feeling and you give the leg."

We laughed. We all laughed. The ice was broken, and it came to me that this man, with no special knowledge, had gone instantly to the heart of the problem—the heart of the *problems*, both his and mine, the comic and basic opposition of positive and negative phantoms. Indeed, he went further:

"This damn phantom," he said. "Stupid bloody thing. Who needs it? Ain't there no way of stopping it happen? By Jiminy," he cried, "*you* are the answer. All they should 'ave done, before they took it off, was to give it an anesthetic, cut the nerves, put it in a cast—so I lost the feeling of it, like you lost yours. And then, when the feeling wasn't there, *then* cut it off! Get rid of the feeling, get rid of the idea, *then* get rid of the thing itself!"

I marveled at this clarity of mind. The idea struck me as sound, even brilliant. I felt like "medicalizing" it for him, and sending a letter in his name to the *Lancet*: "Simple prophylaxis against the development of phantoms."

What I found with him I found with them all. They were all much wiser than the doctors who treated them! There is among doctors, in acute hospitals at least, a presumption of stupidity, in their patients. And *no one* was "stupid," no one is stupid, except the fools who take them as stupid. Working in a chronic hospital, with the same patients, one gains a greater respect for them—for their elemental human wisdom, and the special "wisdom of the heart." But at that first breakfast with my "brothers"—not my colleagues in expertise, but my fellow-patients, fellow-creatures—and throughout my stay in the Convalescent Home, I saw that one must oneself *be* a patient, and a patient among patients, that one must enter both the solitude and the community of patienthood, to have any real idea of what "being a patient" *means*, to understand the immense complexity and depth of feelings, the resonances of the soul in every key—anguish, rage, courage, whatever—and the thoughts evoked, even in the simplest practical minds, because as a patient one's experience *forces* one to think.

Communication in the Home was instant and profound. There was a transparency, a dissolution of the usual barriers, between us. We not only knew the facts about each other (Doc's leg, Mrs. P.'s ovary, etc.), we knew, we sensed, we divined each other's feelings. This sharing of normally hidden and private feelings—feelings, indeed, often hidden from oneself—and the depths of concern and companionship evoked, the giving and sharing of priceless humor and courage—this seemed to be remarkable in the extreme, unlike anything I had ever known and beyond anything I had ever imagined. We had all been through it—sickness and fear—and some of us had walked in the Valley of the Shadow of Death. We had all known the ultimate solitude of being sick and put away, that solitude "which is not threatened in Hell itself." We had all descended to great darknesses and depths—and now we had surfaced, like pilgrims who had taken the same road, but a road, thus far, which had to be traveled alone. The way ahead promised a quite different passage, in which we could be fellow-travelers together.

We had met by chance. We would probably never see each other again. But the meeting, while it lasted, was elemental and profound—an unspoken, shared understanding and sympathy. The certainty, the intuition, of what we shared, the certainty in the depths and foundations of our relations, was like a shared secret which need not be spoken. Indeed, for the most part, our speech was light. We joked, we bantered, we played billiards and banjos, we talked about the news and the latest football scores, and about the flirtations and favoritism we observed in the staff. Everything, on the surface, was merry and light. An outsider would have thought us a frivolous lot, overhearing our conversation. But its lightness, our lightness, covered profound depths. Depth was implied, was secretly present in our words, in the lightest, easiest antics and frolics. If we were frivolous, it was the high spirits of the newborn—and, equally, of those who have known the deepest darkness. But none of this would have been seen by an outsider. He would have observed the surface, not the depths. He would not even have guessed that there *were* any depths concealed and revealed in our frivolities.

After breakfast I wandered out—it was a particularly glorious September morning—settled myself on a stone seat with a large view in all directions, and filled and lit my pipe. This was a new, or at least an almost-forgotten, experience. *I had never had the leisure to light a pipe before*, or not, it seemed to me, for fourteen years at least. Now, suddenly, I had an immense sense of leisure, an unhurriedness, a freedom I had almost forgotten—but which, now it had returned, seemed the most precious thing in life. There was an intense sense of stillness, peacefulness, joy, a pure delight in the "now," freed from drive or desire. I was intensely conscious of each leaf, autumn-tinted, on the ground; intensely conscious of the Eden around me, and, beyond this, the wide sweep of Hampstead

Heath, and the steepled churches of Hampstead and Highgate, high on the skyline. The world was motionless, frozen—everything concentrated in an intensity of sheer being. A perfect peace and communion lay upon the land. This peacefulness had a quality of thanksgiving and praise, a kind of silent, holy intensity; but a silence which was also thanksgiving and song. I felt the grass, the trees, the Heath all round me, the whole earth, all creatures, issuing forth in praise. I felt that all the world itself was one vast hymn—and that my own soul, peaceful, joyful, was part of this hymn.

Everything about me was infinitely familiar. Had I not grown up near Hampstead Heath, and run all over it as a child? It had always been a magic realm, a dearly familiar home. But now, on this morning, as though on the first morning of Creation, I felt like Adam beholding a new world with wonder. I had not known, or had forgotten, that there could be such beauty, such completeness, in every moment. I had no sense at all of "moments," of the serial, only of the perfection and beauty of a timeless "now"—a *nunc stans*.

A magic realm of timelessness had been inserted into time, an intensity of nowness and presentness, of the sort usually devoured by past and future. Suddenly, wonderfully, I found myself exempted from the nagging pressures of past and future and savoring the infinite gift of a complete and perfect now. Idly, but not idle—for in leisure there is neither idleness nor haste—I watched the slow wreathing of smoke, into the still air, from my pipe. Idly I heard, upon every hour, the tolling of bells from all directions: Hampstead calling, tolling, to Highgate, Highgate to Hampstead, each to each, and all to the world.

So I sat, and thought, my mind active, but at peace. And I observed, further, that I was not "unique," and that sitting or strolling in that Paradise were other patients, unhurried, unworried, in repose. All of us were enjoying an extraordinary Sabbath of the spirit—so I guessed, so I confirmed in the sweet and timeless month of my own residence there. There was a peculiar calm, as of a cloister or college, which held us all in its gentle sweet grip. It was for all of us, irrespective of the conditions of our lives, a peculiar interlude unlike anything we had ever known. We had emerged from the sheer misery, the storms and terrors, of sickness, the undermining uncertainty about whether we would get well; but we had not yet been reclaimed by the daily round of life, or of what passes for life in the unredeemed world, with its endless obligations, vexations, expectations. We were being granted a magical interlude, between being-sick and returning-to-the-world, between being-a-patient and being a-paterfamilias-and-breadwinner, between being "in" and being "outside," between past and future. The mood of Saturday morning lasted; it was as undimmed, as radiant, a week, a month later.

Another September, another year, having found peace after a period of fret, I find myself reading Hannah Arendt, on "The gap between past and future: the *nunc stans*." Indeed, this is interleaved in the act of recollection: I recollect and write for a while, and then take a break for Hannah Arendt. She speaks of a "timeless region, an eternal presence in complete quiet, lying beyond human clocks and calendars altogether, the quiet of the Now in the time-pressed, time-tossed existence of man . . . this small non-time space is the very heart of time," and how it is the very home, the only home, of Mind, Soul and Art;

the only point where past and future are gathered together and the pattern and the meaning of the whole become clear. Precisely this timelessness was given now—the special gift of Kenwood.

In my student days, alas, I largely took Oxford for granted, and failed to appreciate or make use of its timelessness, its privilege, but I was vividly aware of my privilege now—the special interlude being granted to me in this time of convalescence. I felt this intensely. Everyone did at the Home. For many—job-ridden, family-ridden, chronically worried and anxious—it was the first real leisure, the first vacation they had ever had—the first time they had ever had time to think—or feel. All of us, in our way, thought deeply at this time and, I suspect, were profoundly changed, sometimes permanently, by the experience.

In the hospital we lost our sense of the world. It was in the Convalescent Home that we first re-encountered the world—albeit at a distance, attenuated, in miniature. My first morning I had spent basking in the sun, going for short exploratory sallies in the garden; I could stroll, with my crutches, for a few minutes at this point. In the afternoon I made it to the gate of the Home. This involved an incline, and knocked me out completely. Gasping, trembling, I sank down by the gate, overwhelmingly reminded of my incapacity and inadequacy. Across the road, in the playing fields of Highgate, I saw the school team practicing rugger, a sight I normally enjoy. I was surprised and appalled at a spasm of hate in myself. I hated their health, their strong young bodies. I hated their careless exuberance and freedom—their freedom from the limitations which I felt, so overwhelmingly, in myself. I looked at them with virulent envy, with the mean rancor, the poisonous spite, of the invalid; and then turned away: I could bear them no longer. Nor could I bear my own feelings, the revealed ugliness of myself.

I consoled myself, after a fashion, by saying, "This is not me—not the real me—but my sickness which is speaking. A well-documented phenomenon—the hateful spite of the sick."

And I added, "You may *feel* it, but be sure you don't *show* it."

Greatly shaken, appalled, I tottered back to my seat. The day was still sunny, but morally overcast.

I had a similar experience the very next day, when as I wandered in the grounds I came across rabbits in a hutch. Again I was surprised by a spasm of hate: "How *dare* they frolic, when *I* am disabled?" And, again, by a beautiful cat, whom I hated precisely for her beauty and grace.

I was appalled by these reactions, this venomous, bilious turning-away from life, these sudden floodings of bile after the exalted, lyrical sentiments I professed. But they were instructive, and it was important to face them; important, too, to *confess* them, for the understanding of others. And here my fellow-patients were marvelous, for when I *did* confess, shamefaced and stuttering, they said, "Don't worry, we went through it ourselves. We all go through it—it'll go away soon."

I hoped they were right. I could not be sure. All I could be certain of was my hate at the time. I smiled, kindly, at the aged and infirm; indeed I could tolerate nobody else. My heart went out to the ailing and suffering, but shut itself with a snap at the spectacle of health.

But on Monday, when I started on the physiotherapy program, and the therapist was affirmative and profoundly encouraging, giving me the feeling that I might hope for a virtually complete recovery, I discovered that the hateful feeling was gone. I stroked the cat, I fed the rabbits, and I spent an hour watching the young footballers with pleasure. Here, then, was a radical turning *to* life.

I find it difficult to write of all this, even years later. It is easy to recollect the good things of life, the times when one's heart rejoices and expands, when everything is enfolded in kindness and love; it is easy to recollect the fineness of life—how noble one was, how generous one felt, what courage one showed in the face of adversity. It is harder to recollect how hateful one has been.

I lied when I said, "It's not me, not the real me. It's the sickness that's speaking." For sickness has no voice, and it *was* me, a nasty me. How can I claim that my goodness, my lofty feelings, constitute the "real me," and that my rancor and malice are just "sickness" and not me?

We can readily see in others what we do not care, or dare, to see in ourselves. The patients I work with are chronically ill. They have, they know they have, little or no hope of recovery. Some of them show a transcendent humor and gallantry, an unspoilt love and affirmation of life. But others are bitter, virulent, envenomed—great haters, great spiters, murderous, demonic. It is not the sickness but the person that shows here, his collapse or corruption with the cruelties of life. If we have youth, beauty, blessed gifts, strength, if we find fame, fortune, favor, fulfillment, it is easy to be nice, to turn a warm heart to the world. But let us be disfavored, disfigured, incapacitated, injured; let us fall from health and strength, from fortune and favor; let us find ourselves ill, miserable and without clear hope of recovery—then our mettle, our moral character, will be tried to the limit.

I was tried myself, but only a little, and even so showed an ugly reaction. It soon went away. I did not have to live with a permanent disability—with a *sense* of permanent disability and misfortune. There was another patient at my table—a young painter who had just come back from open-heart surgery, after years of increasing cardiac disability. He was physically distressed for much of the time, and he looked haggard and aged and had a mean skunk-like look. He was at pains to suppress his feelings of rancor, which added to his miseries, and of which he felt ashamed; but they showed, in his eyes, even when he bit his tongue to keep silent. And *my* feelings to him, not too amiable, must have shown too, because one day he burst out, "It's OK for you. You're getting better. You'll soon be well. You'll be able to do whatever you want. But what do your *doctor's* eyes tell you of me? I've got a bum heart, rotten vessels, the bypass isn't working. Sure, I'll go out, but I'll be back again. I've been here five times. They know me by now. People don't like to look in my face. They see the death-sentence, and that I'm taking it badly. They see my blue lips, and my meanness as well—as you see it, and then pretend you've seen nothing. Not nice, not a pretty sight, not dignified, not fine. But tell me what the hell I do about it, friend?"

Like College, the Convalescent Home had structure and freedom—both, perhaps, in an unusual degree. There were set meal times, and set tables in the refectory for patients, set times for physiotherapy, and other activities, set times for medical visits and, at first, set limits for all other visits. Going out was not permitted to begin with, and when it was it was limited. Permission had to be given, with return by the curfew. And yet, in contrast to these almost monastic restrictions, there was the timelessness, the freedom, the idealism, of a monastery. A single thought or feeling held us together, the long pilgrimage which would finally return us to health and home, a thought at once devotional and practical. This was the unity and center of our lives—and perhaps it was not so far from the thought of a monastery—or, in its best sense, of a university also. We had known sickness as one knows error or evil, and now sought for health, the restored balance of being, as one seeks for goodness or truth.

The daily curriculum, the set limits, were important. Without them we might have drifted into structurelessness and chaos, misjudged our capacities and either lain about, regressively and passively, or pushed ourselves far beyond our capacities. None of us yet had the resilience of health. We were still brittle, precarious; and we needed structure and care. We could not yet physically enjoy the freedom of health, its unthinking carelessness, exuberance and abundance. Thus our daily activities, our lives, had to be measured—and only gradually allowed to approach the normal.

I was constantly escaping and overdoing things myself. I would go for a vast walk in the grounds, lured by the spacious lawns which led downwards, and the great sense of ease in these springy descents—only to find at the bottom, where the brook ran, that I was profoundly exhausted; and as I painfully made my way back I would find strength and tone in the left leg wilt away, and then, for my pains, a massive effusion in the knee which might lay me up, bedridden, for twenty-four hours. There was this sense of deceptive ease—but also of immense effort and difficulty in quite simple matters. It was not easy to get into or out of bed, or to maneuver into position for toilets and chairs. Constantly the crutches had to be at hand, and the yard-long caliper to grasp things at a distance. I found it hard to put on my left sock in the morning. I had to use a peculiar device, which had to be cast, snagged and then drawn on to the foot—like an exercise in fly-fishing.

We had come for convalescence. We had to get better. But getting better is not an automatic and simple process, though getting sick, sickening, may occur by itself. It is significant perhaps that we do not have the corresponding word or concept, "healthening." Instead we have "healing," which means "making whole," which implies, not a process, but an act—many acts.

There is, of course, an automatic recovery—in regard to tissues, for example. This, indeed, was the only meaning of recovery, so far as the surgeon was concerned. Tissues had been severed, tissues had been joined; his job was done, for tissue-healing is automatic. Strictly speaking, *qua* surgeon, *qua* "carpenter," he was right, though there was a sort of grudging prescription for "physiotherapy, post operative," as if this was something purely medical or mechanical. . . .

There was, and is, a mechanical aspect to this. Muscles must be exercised, or they lose strength and tone. Exercise is necessary, and beneficial, for the muscles—necessary, and yet not enough. For standing, walking, let alone more complex motor skills and activities, are not just a matter of muscles (even if, as in my own case, the prime injury be muscular). Rehabilitation involves action, *acts*. Rehabilitation must be centered on the character of acts— and how to call them forth, when they have come apart, disintegrated, been "lost"—or "forgotten." Without this I would, indeed, have remained bed-ridden—precisely as Hippocrates says.

But I could not do this by will-power, or on my own steam, alone. The initiation, the impulse, had to come from without. I had to *do* it, give birth to the New Act, but others were needed to deliver me, and *say*, "Do it!" They were the permitters, the prescribers, the midwives of the act—and, of course, its supporters and encouragers, And this was not just neurosis or passivity. Every patient, no matter how strong-minded or strong-willed, encounters precisely the same difficulty in taking his first step, in doing (or re-doing) anything anew. He cannot conceive it—"the imagination is subdued"—and others, under-standing, must tip him into action. They (inter)mediate, so to speak, between passivity and action.

This was the supreme act, the high point, of recovery. But it was not the end, only the beginning. And if I had to spend another six weeks thereafter, it was because other acts were needed, of a similar kind, because the restoration of higher function is not smooth and automatic. Rehabili-tation, in this way, is recapitulation, second childhood; for, like childhood, it involves decisive acts of learning, sudden ascents from one level to the next, each level in-conceivable to the level below. Physiology, or at least the physiology of higher functions, is dependent upon, em-bedded in, experiences and acts, and unless experiences and acts are made possible—the essential role of the therapist or teacher—the nervous system, the organization, will neither mature nor heal.

Thus, in the Convalescent Home, though I grew daily stronger, and could do the same things with ever-greater power and ease, I could not do anything different, or new. This always required the intervention of another. This was shown, very strikingly, when the time came for me to "graduate"—to one crutch, and then, later, to a cane.

There was a particularly fine and understanding young surgeon who visited the Convalescent Home three times a week, a man who understood, and with whom communication was possible. I once asked him about this (I *could* ask him such a question, where I could ask nothing, or almost nothing, of my surgeon in the hospital).

"It's simple," he replied, "Maybe you guessed the answer. *I've been through this myself.* I had a broken leg. . . . *I know what it's like.*"

So, when Mr. Amundsen said that the time had come to graduate, and give up one crutch, he spoke with authority—the only real authority, that of experience and understanding. I believed him. I had faith in him. But what he suggested was—impossible.

"It's impossible," I stammered. "I can't imagine it."

"You don't have to 'imagine' it, only to *do* it."

Nerving myself up, quivering with tension, I tried—and immediately tripped and fell flat on my face. I tried again—and fell flat again.

"Don't worry," he said. "It'll just *come*—you'll see."

(It "came" later that day—but it came in a *dream.*)

It was at this time that I received a phone call from

a friend. There was to be an anniversary service in Westminster Abbey for W. H. Auden—could I come? I loved and revered Auden, I wanted to come. More, I felt a duty to pay my last respects. I was painfully conflicted, but the terror won out:

"I'm terribly sorry," I said. "Of course I would come if it were physically possible. But at this stage, I'm afraid, it's completely unthinkable. I so wish I could come, but it's not to be thought of." Yes, these were the words, the very words, I used.

The next morning the physiotherapist looked in to see me—she had seen the proofs on my table of an article I had written on Auden—and remarked, "They said it was a deeply moving ceremony in the Abbey. *You* tell me all about it—of course you were there."

I was thunderstruck. My mental world seemed to shake. "But," I stammered, "I couldn't go."

"Why not?" she demanded.

"I was asked to, I wanted to, but it was unthinkable, not to be thought of."

"Unthinkable!" she exploded. "Not to be thought of? *Of course*, you could have gone. You should have gone. What the hell stopped you? Why shouldn't you go out?"

My God, she was right! Who stopped me, what stopped me? What nonsense I had uttered about "not to be thought of." The moment she spoke and said "Why not?" a great barrier disappeared—though I had not thought of it as a barrier, just "not to be thought of." Was I "prohibited"—or was "the imagination subdued?"

Whatever it was, I was liberated by her words, and said, "Godammit, I am going out right now!"

"Good," she replied. "And high time, too."

Swiftly, unthinkingly, I strode out of the gate and up the hill to Highgate. Wonderful! Ecstasy! My first walk outside. Until this walk, this moment, going outside had been "unthinkable"—I had felt an inmate and an invalid, and couldn't imagine it otherwise. I had been completely unable to take this crucial step. Stepping outside into the wide world needed her "Why not?"

I found a little teashop, at the top of Highgate Hill, and boldly, unhesitatingly, went in for tea.

"You made it," said the waitress. "You finally made it here."

"Do you know me?" I asked, amazed.

"I don't know you personally," she said. "*I know how it is*. You folks sit in the Convalescent Home till you're ready to explode—and, all of a sudden, you *do* explode, and the explosion takes you up the steep hill to Highgate, and right to this teashop, for your first meal outside!"

"Yes," I said, "you're right on all counts."

And then I ordered myself, not just a pot of tea, but a veritable feast to celebrate my release.

"They all do that!" the waitress declared.

"They all," "You all." What did I care? Indeed it pleased me that I had acted, evidently, as many others before me. It made me feel less apart, less alienated, or "unique": it placed me in the common rut, among others, a part of the world.

I ordered almost everything on the menu—from anchovy toast to rum-balls and meringues—and everything was marvelous, the very food of love (oral music). Not only marvelous, but holy—I felt the meal as a sacrament, my first communion with the world. I had been starved of the world, now, for more than six weeks. I was hungry for the world, and I felt it as a feast. With every sacred mouthful—and I ate slowly, though hugely, with thanksgiving and reverence—I felt I was partaking of that holy feast, the world. The substance, the sensuousness, was spiritual as well. The food and drink were blessed—a sacramental feast.

From this moment there was no stopping me. I went out constantly, I fell in love with the world, I chartered taxis as extravagantly as a potentate visiting from another land. And, in a sense, this is what I felt like—a man, a king, long exiled, returning, accorded a wonderful, royal welcome by the world he was returning to. I wanted to hug familiar dear buildings; I wanted to hug chance strangers in the street—to hug them, devour them, like my first meal in the teashop—for they too were part of the wonderful feast. I must have smiled and laughed a great deal, or otherwise exuded happiness and love, because I received a great deal in return. I felt this especially in the pubs around Hampstead—wonderful, jolly, crowded pubs, with gardens and awnings bright in the warm sun, and people the most genial and congenial in the world. My crutches (for I needed both, to get in and out of taxis), my cast, served as a passport of universal validity. I was welcomed, I was made much of, wherever I went. And I loved it, I who had been so withdrawn and so shy. I found myself singing, playing darts, telling bawdy stories, laughing.

Everywhere, and in myself, I discovered a Rabelaisian gusto—a coarse, but festive, and perfectly chaste gusto. But also, and equally, I sought for the byways of life, quiet glades, moonlit walks, for meditation. I wanted to give thanks, in every mode—in energy, in quietude; in company, alone; with friends, with strangers; in action, in thought. The joy of this time was extraordinarily intense—but it seemed to me a healthy joy, without mania or sickness. I felt that this was how one *should* find the world—how the world really was, if one were not jaded or tarnished. I felt the gaiety and innocence of the newborn.

And if this was "the truth," or how things should be, how could one find the world *dull*? I wondered if what one normally calls "normal" was itself a sort of dullness, a deadening of sense and spirit, if not, indeed, a very closure of their doors. For myself, now, liberated, released, emergent from the dark night and abyss, there was an intoxication of light and love and health.

I felt that a profound crisis had occurred in my life, and that from now on I would be profoundly and permanently transformed. I would take less for granted—indeed nothing for granted. I would see life, all being, as the most precious of gifts, infinitely vulnerable and precarious, to be infinitely prized and cherished.

On Monday, October the 7th—six weeks after my operation—I was taken back to the hospital, to be checked and uncasted—uncasted for good, if all was well. I had no fear, I knew all was well—and I wanted to see my once-cursed surgeon and his team in an amicable light.

Happily this occurred, and presented no problem. Mr. Swan found himself faced with a beaming grateful patient, who showed nothing but affability and regrets for past ire. He could not but respond in kind to all this, though his response had a quality of shyness and reserve. He smiled, but not widely; he shook my hand, but not warmly; he was cordial, but not amiable. I marveled that I could have endowed him with such hatefulness before—for he wasn't really hateable, any more than he was lovable: just a decent, quiet man, professional and reserved; technically admirable, I had never doubted this at any time, but uncomfortable with the realities of powerful emotions, and incapable of meeting emotional demands—at least, demands as extreme as I had made, in my anguish. Now my anguish was over and my apprehensions were stilled, now I was *better*, I made no demands—and this pleased him greatly, and allowed a faint smile. As he changed for me, doubtless I changed for him. I imagined him chatting with the "team" later: "Not a bad chap, that Sacks—a bit emotional, of course. He was a bit of a nuisance in hospital, mind you—but maybe it was a difficult time for him. Wouldn't care to be in that situation myself. But he's fine now, isn't he? Leg looks splendid. All's well that ends well." And with this he would dismiss me from his mind.

Yes, indeed, with the cast off, my leg did look splendid—it had fleshed out handsomely, though it was still thinner (and somewhat cooler) than the other one, and the surgical scar was neat and trim—and handsome, too, in its way, especially if I thought of it as a battle scar, heroic. There was none of the alienation which had so shocked me four weeks before. The leg was clearly alive, clearly real, clearly flesh, clearly mine, with only a slight vagueness or oddness about the knee. I was somewhat surprised, therefore, to find the skin numb—absolutely numb, anaesthetic, throughout the whole area where the cast had been. It wasn't a deep numbness—proprioception seemed normal (which went with the normal, unalienated feel of the limb)—but a dense, superficial one.

As I returned to Kenwood in the ambulance I rubbed

and kneaded the leg in my hands; and as I did so, as I stimulated the skin and its sensors, sensation came back, minute by minute, and had almost completely returned in the hour of the trip. Whether it was the deprivation of ordinary sensations inside the cast, or the pressure of the plaster, I wasn't sure. I found that other patients had found similar numbness—superficial, transient, and seemingly not of much account. The loss of deep sensation, of proprioception, was quite different, and deadly. . . .

I say "almost," because one area, on the outside of my thigh and knee, didn't yield to my ministrations and remained totally without any sensation whatever. This was where the skin branches of the femoral nerve had been cut in the operation.

Now the cast was off, a final problem remained—getting some movement at the knee, which seemed immovably rigid, transfixed in extension by a huge mass of scar tissue. I had to spend half an hour each day forcefully, forcibly, making the knee bend, trying to loosen up and break down the hard fibrous scar.

On Friday, since all was going well, I was permitted to spend a night at home. The whole family gathered to welcome me—it was Sabbath Eve. The next morning, I went to the synagogue with my father and brothers, and we were all called up together for the reading of the law. And this, to my surprise, was an inexpressible joy; for behind my family I felt embraced by a community and, behind this, by the beauty of old traditions, and, behind this, by the ultimate, eternal joy of the law. The portion was from Genesis, near the beginning, most appropriate to a man who felt reborn; for shortly before, on Simchat

Torah—The Rejoicing of the Law—the year-long reading of the law had come to its end, and restarted, and the shofar had been blown, followed by a great cry: "Now the world is new created."

The service, the ceremonies, the Bible stories, now made sense—in a way which they had never fully or truly done before. A pantheistic feeling had infused the past month, the feeling that the world was God's gift, to be thanked back to God. Now, within the religious ceremonies and stories, I found a true parable of my own experience and condition—the experience of affliction and redemption, darkness and light, death and rebirth—the "pilgrimage" which fortune, or my injury, had forced upon me. Now, as never before, I found relevance in the scriptural symbols and stories. I felt that my own story had the shape of such a universal existential experience, the journey of a soul into the underworld and back, a spiritual drama—on a neurological basis.

In a sense my experience had been a religious one— I had certainly thought of the leg as exiled, God-forsaken, when it was "lost" and, when it was restored, restored in a transcendental way. It had, equally, been a riveting scientific and cognitive experience—but it had transcended the limits of science and cognition. I felt it likely that this would effect a permanent change, and dispose me sympathetically to philosophy and religion, without abating a jot my scientific passion and rigor. I saw, I foresaw, how they would come together in me.

Another twelve days and I was discharged from Kenwood, an exemplary convalescent judged fit for the world. I had loved it there and formed real bonds with others, and saying farewell was a poignant experience, which resounded with its original and proper meaning. We had journeyed together, for a brief but profound portion of life; we had shared our feelings with a rare intimacy and candor; and now we were parting and going our ways, wishing each other to fare well on the journey of life.

I had known great happiness and great peace at Kenwood, but it was an interlude in life, and so had to have its end. I was still not wholly functional, and I felt I wanted another opinion—from some experienced orthopedist who would look at me with fresh eyes and give me advice for the future.

I phoned Mr. W.R. of Harley Street, who said he would see me the next day.

I presented myself hopefully, but with no particular expectations. He was a ruddy, genial man, who immediately put me at my ease, and listened with attention, occasionally asking a penetrating question. He gave me the sense that he was interested in *me*—me as a person, no less than as a problem; and he seemed to have all the time in the world, though I knew he was one of the most sought-after men in England. He listened, with perfect concentration and courtesy, and then he examined me, swiftly, but authoritatively, in detail.

This is a master, I said to myself: I will listen to him as he has listened to me.

"Quite an experience, Dr. Sacks," he concluded. "Ever consider making it into a book?"

I was flustered, and flattered, and said that I had.

"The alienation," he continued, "—it's a common phenomenon. I often see it in my patients, and I warn them beforehand."

Here was a master indeed, I thought. Would things have been different if *HE* had been my surgeon?

"In your case, of course, the alienation was worse, because of the profound proprioceptive deficit. I can still demonstrate this, at the knee, though it is no longer symptomatic. But you may get symptoms if you push the leg too hard. You will have to exercise judgment for a year, at the least.

"Now, as regards your walking, and as regards your knee, you walk as if you still had the cast. You hold the leg stiffly, as if you had no knee. Yet you have 15 degrees of flexion already—not much, but enough. Enough to walk normally if only you *used* it."

I nodded assent.

"Why do you walk as if there were no knee? It is partly habit—this is how you walked with the cast—partly, I think, because you have 'forgotten' your knee, and can't imagine what using it is like."

"I know," I said. "I feel that myself. But I can't seem to use it in a deliberate way. Whenever I try, it feels awkward. I stumble."

He thought for a moment. "What do you like doing?" he continued. "What comes to you naturally? What is your favorite physical activity?"

"Swimming," I answered, with no hesitation.

"Good," he said. "I have an idea." There was a half-smile, somewhat impish, on his face. "I think your best plan is to go for a swim. Will you excuse me for a minute? I have a phone call to make."

He came back in a minute, the smile more pronounced.

"A taxi will be here in five minutes," he said. "It will take you to a pool. I'll see you at the same time tomorrow."

The taxi arrived, and took me to the Seymour Hall Baths. I rented a towel and trunks, and advanced tremblingly to the side. There was a young lifeguard there, lounging by the diving board, who looked at me quizzically and said, "Why, what's the matter?"

"I've been told I ought to take a swim," I said. "The doctor told me, but I'm disabled. I've had surgery, I'm sort of scared."

The lifeguard unwound himself, slowly, languidly, leaned towards me, looked mischievous and suddenly said "Race you!", at the same time taking my stick with his right hand and pushing me in with his left.

I was in the water, outraged, before I knew what had happened—and then the impertinence, the provocation, had their effect. I am a good swimmer—a "natural"—and have been since childhood—from infancy, indeed, for my father, a swimming-champ, had thrown us in at six months, when swimming is instinctual and doesn't have to be learnt. I felt challenged by the lifeguard. By God, I'd show him! Provocatively he stayed just a little in front of me, but I kept up a fast crawl for four Olympic lengths, and only stopped then because he yelled "Enough!"

I got out of the pool—and found I walked normally. The knee was now working, it had "come back" completely.

When I saw Mr. W.R. the next day, he gave a big laugh and said "Splendid!"

He asked me the details, I told him and he laughed even more.

"Good Lad!" he said. "He does it just the right way."

I realized then that the whole scene, the scenario, was *his* doing, *his* suggestion—that he had *told* the lifeguard precisely what to do. I burst out laughing too.

"Damnedest thing," he said. "It always seems to work. What one needs is spontaneity, to be *tricked* into action. And you know," he leaned forward, "it's the same with a dog!"

"A dog?" I repeated, stupidly blinking.

"Yes, a dog," he replied. "It happened with mine—Yorkshire terrier, sweet bitch, broke her silly leg. I set it, it healed perfectly, but she'd only walk on three legs—kept sparing the broken one, had forgotten how to use it. It went on for two months. She *wouldn't* walk properly. So I took her down to Bognor, and waded out to sea, carrying this stupid sweet animal with me. I took her out as far as I could, and then dumped her in and let her swim back. She swam back with a strong symmetrical paddle, and then scampered off along the beach on *all four legs*. Same therapy in both cases—unexpectedness, spontaneity, somehow evoking a natural action."

I was delighted with this story, and with Mr. W.R. generally. I was rather pleased to be compared with a dog—I much preferred it to being called "unique." And it brought home something about the elemental nature of the animal soul and animal motion, and about spontaneity, musicality, animation.

Spontaneity! That was it! But how could one plan spontaneity? It was almost a contradiction in terms. Spontaneity, playfulness, it was comically clear, lay at the heart of W.R.'s theory and practice of therapy—the finding of some activity which was natural and meaningful, an expression of a will that found delight in itself—"*condelectari sibi*" in Duns Scotus' words. "What do you enjoy?" he had said. "What gives you delight?" W.R.'s therapy was essentially "Scotian"—and he had arrived, intuitively, at the point of view that all function is embedded in action, and that acting, therefore, is the key to all therapy—be it playful, earnest, impulsive, spontaneous, musical, theatrical, so long as it is action.

The next day I went to our local pool in Kilburn—the pool my father had thrown me into, forty years before—and had a delectable Scotian swim, so full of delight that I could have gone on forever—for in activity which is joyful, as opposed to activity that is labor, there is no drive, no exhaustion, only delight and repose. Leaving the pool at last, not exhausted but refreshed, I saw the bus I wanted rounding a corner. Without thinking, just responding, I ran after it, caught it, jumped onto it and ran up the stairs. And there were another two victories for Scotus—I had not known I could run or jump, and had I tried, deliberately, I would have come to grief. Indeed that very morning I said mournfully to myself, "You can walk, my boy, but you'll never run or jump."

On Friday evening I took myself off, profanely, to the Cricklewood dance hall. I watched with delight the dancers dancing—contrasting this with my sourness five weeks before, when I had turned away in hate from the young footballers at Highgate. I felt the itch, the impulse, to dance myself, but I would not have dared to do so—me, a middle-aged man, just out of a cast—if a bunch of dancers hadn't grabbed my arm and gaily forced me to join their rhythm. I didn't have to think. I had no decision to make, I was caught up in joyful motion, natural will—*ut natura*—before I realized what was happening.

I slept late the next morning, and didn't wake up till my brother came in, saying "Here's a letter from your pal Professor Luria in Moscow."

I took the letter from him, trembling with excitement. It had been seven weeks since I had written to Luria, feeling that he, and he only, would understand what I wrote. I had been fearful when weeks passed without a reply, for he had always responded promptly when I had written to him before (but the delay was benign, he had been in his summer *dacha*). What would he say? He would certainly say what he felt. He was incapable of dissimulation, as he was incapable of grossness. Would he say, delicately, that I had been hysterical, mad? I tore open the letter, afraid of my own thoughts.

Yes, yes, dear God, he believed me! He believed what I was saying—and found it "most important!" He found my observations surprising, yet ultimately coherent—with the unity one would expect, given the functional unity of the organism. He felt I was really "discovering a new field" and that it was vital that I tell my story.

Ah, what a letter! The most beautiful, understanding, generous letter in the world! A letter of salutation—and profound affirmation. A letter which gratified my dearest, deepest wishes; but, precisely because these were grounded in reality: in science, philosophy, love of truth, wish and reality became one.

Drunk with happiness, I found myself walking to the Heath. In childhood, Hampstead Heath had been my playground and dreamscape—the favored place of all my childhood fantasies and games. As an adolescent and a young man, I had fallen in love with it again. Here, more sedately, I would walk and talk with my friends, timelessly, all day. More important perhaps, Hampstead Heath was later the scene of long meditative rambles, when the childish fancies became the scientific dreams and theories of the young man.

I walked to Parliament Hill, one of the highest points, commanding fine vistas in every direction. I thought of all that had passed in the previous nine weeks—the immense adventure, now drawing to its close. I had seen depths and heights not commonly seen. I had dwelt in them, explored them, the far limits of experience. Now, in a sense, I would come down to earth, would be leading a more normal and ordinary life, without the wild extremities and epiphanies of the past weeks. I felt this as a loss. My adventure was ending. But I knew that something momentous had happened, which would leave its mark, and alter me, decisively, from now on. A whole life, a whole universe, had been compressed into these weeks: a density of experience neither given to, nor desired by, most men; but one which, having happened, would refashion and direct me.

"I am sorry it happened to you," wrote Luria, "but if such a thing happens it can only be understood, and used. Perhaps it was your destiny to have the experience; certainly it is your duty now to understand and explore . . . Really you are opening and discovering a new field."

CHAPTER SEVEN

THE LONG ROAD

The truth of things is after all their living fulness, and some day, from a more commanding point of view than was possible to any one in [a previous] generation, our descendants, enriched with the spoils of all our analytic investigations, will get round to that higher and simpler way of looking at nature.

—William James

A curious excitement possessed me—I had to go to the book fair in Boston, I had to get the Henry Head, those wonderful volumes in green and red cloth; for in them, somewhere, was "the answer."

I had seen them months before, at the book fair in Toronto, kept picking them up, then putting them down, with a strange and peremptory feeling of *"not yet."* This time there was no hesitation. I walked straight to the stall, and, yes, they were there! I had the strongest sense that they had been waiting for me.

The bookseller smiled: "I knew you'd be back. I saw it in Toronto. I knew you'd be back for Head." He knew it, and, unconsciously, I knew it too. Head had been waiting for me for many years, and now I had come back to him, the prodigal son, finally seeing the tradition to which I belonged. I bought the books at once and decided to take the train back to New York, the slowest train possible, one which would ramble through the countryside. I wanted a long and slow journey, so that I could read Head without interruption. For Head, I now knew, would be the occasion of understanding, of suddenly seeing, as from a mountaintop, very clear, in perspective, spread out before me, the as-yet uncollected and uncohered thoughts of many years.

Luria had spoken to me of discovering "a new field," and of "the long road"—arduous, singular, indirect— which was the only route to it. He had spoken of the long and tortuous groping in the dark, and of the beauty, the simplicity of understanding, when it was found.

> The years of searching in the dark for a truth that one feels but cannot express, the intense desire and the alternations of confidence and misgiving until one breaks through the clarity and understanding are known only to him who has himself experienced them.
>
> —Einstein

Now, at last, the illumination would come; it would come with reading Henry Head on this jolting train, as it passed through tiny New England villages and the blazing maples of late fall, under an infinite autumnal sky.

I had not read Head since my student days, but now, with the sudden pounce of the sleepwalker, I found precisely the passage I needed in a chapter called "Chaos," in the volume *Aphasia*: "The complete act in its perfect form demands the mobilization in due sequence of a series of complex procedures; here the time relation . . . is of

fundamental importance. A want of chronological exactitude will throw the whole movement into disorder; *its
'kinetic melody' has been destroyed.*"

I read the passage again and again, altering the
emphasis with each reading, sensing more and more a
doubleness, as if two modes of thought, two realms, had
conjoined. On the one hand, there was the language of
analysis, science, and neurology: "sequence," "series,"
"complex procedures," all needing to be mobilized with
"chronological exactitude." On the other hand, Head
spoke of "completeness," "wholeness," "perfection," and
"melody," the language of the visionary, the poet. And as
I pondered this I remembered what my father, who was
Head's resident sixty-five years ago, had often said of him:
"He was the most rigorous of scientists, but he was a poet
too. He *felt* the music of movement and speech, but as a
neurologist he could not *explain* it."

The abstracting and analyzing mind breaks up movement, sees it as a sequence, a series of complex procedures.
The intuitive, esthetic sensibility perceives it as continuous,
indivisible, a stream akin to melody.

My father often spoke of Head's passion for theory,
and how this conflicted with his feeling for life. How, with
a certain melancholy, he would quote the famous lines
from *Faust*:

> *Grau, theurer Freund, ist all Theorie
> Und grün des Lebens goldner Baum.*

"Neurology is grey, a grey science, my friend," he would
say to my father as they worked in the clinic, "and outside
is the green and golden tree of life."

Head was not alone in his predicament. Perhaps it was the predicament of science itself. And here, following on the remembrance of Head, I thought of some words of great pathos in Darwin, in which he describes the effect of science, the scientific habit, on himself:

> I have almost lost my taste for pictures or music. . . . My mind seems to have become a sort of machine for grinding general laws out of large collections of fact. . . . The loss of these tastes, this curious and lamentable loss of the higher aesthetic tastes, is a loss of happiness, and may possibly be injurious to the intellect . . . and more probably to the moral character, by enfeebling the emotional part of our nature.

But must one repudiate or repress "the higher esthetic tastes," "the emotional part of our nature," in the service of science? Must there always be an irreconcilable gap? Head, my father thought, had had the passionate, though unrealized, desire to transcend it. And occasionally, in rare passages, more often in conversation, he would find a way to fuse thought and feeling. But it was very rare, and, as he himself used to say, "It is not yet the time."

Now I put down the heavy green volume of *Aphasia*, and picked up the crimson *Studies in Neurology*. Indeed, this was what I had intended to read in the first place. So with great intentness, and a sense of our kinship—with the countryside rolling past and the iron wheels rolling under me—I travelled through the *Studies*, delighted by the neurological landscape, by the intellectual movement which everywhere suffused it. But soon I was also disconcerted by Head's formal viewpoint, which amounted to a presentation of the patient and physician as entirely passive; and of neurology and medicine as just a mechanical iteration of tests and tasks.

When I first became a doctor and decided to enter neurology, there was a part of me that wanted only the pure joy and challenge of concepts—abstractions divorced from any human reality. This, I think, is not uncommon among neurologists: They have a reputation, not entirely undeserved, for being "brainy" and heartless in equal degree. It was safer, "cleaner," to keep a distance from patients, to keep from entering their strange and often terrifying world. In "pure" medicine, the questions of existence, deep and terrible, were neatly excluded. This was "safe"—but it was also a sort of death, a cutting-off from the rich phenomenality of experience, the phenomena of sickness and health alike.

From this secure but death-like stupor, the experiences of *Awakenings* served to awaken me. But there was still a distance to be travelled, for though I tried with all the imagination and empathy I could muster to enter, to realize, the experiences of my patients, I was finally, organically, unable to do so. One cannot "imagine" Parkinsonism without *being* Parkinsonian—there is no substitute for experience, a matter on which Montaigne, Einstein and Kant all agreed. Thus, going through all the specific experiences of "The Leg," as well as the more general experiences of "Being a Patient," taught me, changed me, as nothing else could. Now I *knew*, for I had experienced myself. And now I could truly begin to understand my patients, the many hundreds of patients with profound disturbances of body-image and body-ego, whom

I saw over the years. I could listen to them, I could understand them, and sometimes I could help, because I had
traversed this region myself. I came to realize, as did my
patients, that there is an absolute and categorical differ-
ence between a doctor who *knows* and one who does not,
and that this knowing can only be obtained by a personal
experience of the organic, by descending to the very depths
of disease and dissolution.

> To become a true doctor, the candidate must have passed
> through all the illnesses that he wants to cure and all the
> accidents and circumstances that he is to diagnose. Truly
> I should trust such a man. For the others guide us like the
> man who paints seas, reefs, and ports while sitting at his
> table, and sails the model of a ship there in complete
> safety. Throw him into the real thing, and he does not
> know how to go at it.
>
> —Montaigne

I *had* been thrown into "the real thing," and now I did
know how to go at it. And go at it I did, for several years.
Allowing my patients to speak fully and freely, unconfined
by any neurological catechism, I received, again and again,
descriptions of an emotional and existential intensity
almost never to be found in the neurological literature.
Every patient with a severe disturbance of body-perception
or "afferent field" had an equally severe disturbance in his
conceptions, in "body-image"; and every disturbance of
body-image was felt as an equally severe disturbance of
self, or "body-ego." Far from being unique," it became
clear that my own experiences had been typical, exemplary.
Like myself, every such patient went through a profound
ontological experience—dissolutions or de-realizations of

being in the affected areas, associated with an elemental anxiety and horror; followed (if they were fortunate enough to recover) by an equally elemental sense of "re-realization" and joy. Every such experience, to use the medieval term, was an *experimentum suitatis*—a fundamental, if involuntary, experiment in identity.

"Such syndromes are perhaps common," Luria wrote, "but very uncommonly described." Yes, they were indeed common—this was now clear to me; but why were they so uncommonly described? My experience here was almost identical with what I had found, years before, when I came to read up on migraine. I found the current literature virtually empty, either making no observations whatever, or failing to give its observations any depth. Similarly in the realm of "body-image," every patient given a spinal anesthetic feels he has been cut bizarrely in half; that his lower half is "*gone*" and will never come back. This is known to hundreds of thousands of patients; but it is entirely unknown in the medical literature, and apparently to the doctors who give the anesthetics. Thus, as I had done with migraine, I found I needed to go back to the early days when there was still a vivid natural history, a naturalistic description of disease and disorder, as yet unspoiled by concepts.

As I gazed out over rural New England, the little churches and villages scarcely changed since Civil War days, I thought of Weir Mitchell, called rather ponderously "The Father of American Neurology" but in reality a delightful naturalist of health and disorder.

Weir Mitchell had been first to identify "phantom

limbs" (originally calling them "sensory ghosts") and their opposites, the "reflex paralysis," the "negative phantoms," the alienation, the nothingness, which I had experienced and then studied in such detail. He was also the first to realize, by an intense imaginative empathy with his patients —fearfully wounded soldiers in the "stump" hospital in Philadelphia—how a profound "egoistic" dissolution could occur. He described this in what he called a "true clinical fiction"—*The Case of George Dedlow*—which was about a physician who suffered amputation of his limbs. As Dedlow tells us:

> I found to my horror that at times I was less conscious of myself, of my own existence, than used to be the case. The sensation was so novel that it quite bewildered me. Well aware of how absurd I might seem, I refrained from speaking of my case, and strove more keenly to analyze my feelings. . . . It was, as well as I can describe it, a deficiency in the egoistic sentiment of individuality.

Writing during the Civil War, sixty years before Head's concept of body-image, Mitchell goes on to ascribe these feelings, these profound and specific deficiencies of body-image, to "the eternal silence . . . of the great ganglia subserving the limbs." (It is interesting that Mitchell published this as a "clinical fiction" before venturing on his famous "medical" delineations of phantoms. Perhaps he felt that non-medical readers would be willing to consider matters which would be rejected as fanciful by his colleagues.)

But if Weir Mitchell was the first neurologist to describe such disorders, he was also one of the last. A naturalistic neurology, as existed in his time, was still open and accessible to the singularities of experience, the richness of the phenomenal in health and disease. But by the 1880s, with the rise of scientific neurology and its new and powerful mechanical concepts of "function," the possibilities of such naturalism were decisively closed.

Hughlings Jackson was one of the founders of this new vision of the nervous systems as a machine. All is mechanical in Jackson's view—nothing is spontaneous or alive. The other founder was Sherrington, whose initiation into the field came when, as a young man, he saw in a dog with its cerebral hemispheres removed, pure and mechanical reflex reactions unaffected by any interfering "self," or "will." Sherrington called these preparations "Cartesian trigger-puppets," and he devoted his life to their study. Thus Jacksonian and Sherringtonian science *is* "puppet-ology"—a purely mechanical vision of man and creature as reflex puppet.

I withdrew now from musing and gazing as the train pulled into a siding, and returned to Head's *Studies in Neurology*. I travelled with him the long road he had travelled—a road so similar to and yet so different from my own. He too had started at the periphery, he too had been both observer and subject—analyzing the experience of a cut nerve in his arm. And from this he had gone to higher and higher levels of integration in the nervous system, the ways by which the moving body may "know" and modulate itself. Sherrington had spoken of "proprioception," defining it, metaphorically, as "a sixth sense" by which information from moving muscles and joints is gathered and relayed to higher parts of the brain. Head studied this clinically, in patients with various disorders of proprioception, seeing the culmination of this sensory information as an internal model of the body which he came to call the "body image." I leafed through the pages, searching for something akin to my own experience, and I came across this passage:

> The patient was entirely unable to recognize the position into which his lower limbs had been placed passively. Extensive movements could be made to the ankles, knees and hips without his knowledge. If his eyes were closed, the legs could be moved from the extended position in any direction, and the knees flexed to forty degrees, and he still imagined they lay stretched before him on the bed. When he was allowed to open his eyes, his expression of surprise amply testified to the greatness of his error.

A beautiful description—how precisely it recalled my own experience when I asked Nurse Sulu to move my leg! Yes, it was absolutely right, but there was something *missing*. These were impeccable observations from the "outside," but they made no reference to experience, to the "inside." What about the experiencing, suffering patient? *How* did he feel and *what* did he feel? The strangeness of the experience is hinted at: He "imagined" the legs were elsewhere, and he evinced great "surprise." My own guess is that his feelings were far more intense. I suspect he was staggered by the experience; that he found it terrifying and uncanny; and that he found himself entertaining the most extreme and unspeakable doubts about the *reality* of his "lost" legs. But none of this comes through in Head's description, for all he is concerned with is the study of capacity, or "function"—very much as it might be studied in a defective machine.

As long as Head confines himself to the examination

of mechanism and "function," something vital and extraordinary eludes his descriptions. But let him forget his neurological studies and terms for a moment, and give us the actual words of the patient (they are rare, only a handful in the whole volume)—and something infinitely more compelling emerges. Thus I pounced on the words of a patient who complained that "his right leg felt exactly as if it were a cork leg"; and those of a Lieutenant W., who crashed in an aeroplane and realized he had injured his spine because ". . . he felt he had a head and shoulders only."

Philosophically, existentially, such statements are startling, but Head only mentions them in passing, and fails to see their significance. Or does he? My father, who worked closely with him, told me that he was "full of curiosity and sympathy," and would be "fascinated" by the strangeness of what his patients would sometimes tell him. But it is precisely this "fascination" which is missing from the *Studies*. He fails to see the anguish of such statements. For Head, as a Jacksonian, a Sherringtonian, cannot *admit* such experiences in his work—and if he does, it is very rarely, and he never accords them any central emphasis or importance.

I put the book down, exasperated and puzzled. What a fool Head was; how could he miss what was so essential, these experiences from the depths about "identity" and "reality"? But Head was not a fool, he was a most gifted man *of his time*, but as he himself, half-unconsciously, knew, this was *not yet the time* for neurologists to study such matters of "identity" or "reality," even if these were brought up spontaneously by the patient. Head was not given to metaphysical speculation—his genius was strictly active and practical. And if this would have been so of Henry Head, how could it not be so of my surgeons, who were pre-eminently practical men, strictly confined to observing gross structure and function.

To be deaf to metaphysical implication is one thing, but to be deaf to anguish is another; and this was my indictment of classical neurology. It explained my doubling of despair when I was a patient and complained like Head's patients that my leg felt "unreal," only to be told by my doctors: "That's not our business." I saw very clearly, going through the fifteen hundred pages of Head on the train, that classical neurology has no room for such matters, and will not admit them, except as occasional, colorful "figures of speech."

I guessed as much when I was a patient in hospital, hence my urgent sense that another sort of science might hear me—a science represented by Luria, and his field, neuropsychology. And in this hope, both at the time of my illness and in the years that followed, when scarcely a week passed without correspondence with Luria, I was to be both gratified and disappointed.

As a patient in hospital I felt both anguish and asphyxia— the anguish of being confronted with dissolution, and asphyxia because I could not be heard. In my despair I turned to Luria; who wrote at the close of his first letter to me: "Please publish your observations. It may do something to alter the 'veterinary' approach to peripheral disorders." I had already been favorably disposed to neuropsychology in general and Luria in particular—and now his letter won me over completely, coming, as it did, in answer to my anguish, and filled, equally, with intellectual penetration and human warmth. In Darwin's *Biography of an Infant*, one feels that science and affection are conjoined, that "Darwin the scientist" and "Darwin the father" are one and the same, and that this is the ideal of a true and humane science. So in Luria's letter—I felt that science and concern were conjoined, were indivisible, in the ideal of a humane medicine. This filled me with gratitude, with wonder, with hope—coming after the despair of non-communication with my surgeons, and the experience of a medicine which had treated me as a thing. As the coldness and the blindness of a "puppet" medicine were one, so the warmth and the insight of a "person" medicine were one. This was the lesson of Luria's letter; and it would be, I thought, the lesson of neuropsychology—the new science he had done so much to create. I failed to realize how Luria himself had humanized his science; and it was only after his death that the impersonality of his method and the science was revealed. It was similar, my father told me, when Head retired from science—as he was forced to, prematurely, by the most severe Parkinsonism. In Head's presence, neurology seemed warm, but without Head's great personal charm and warmth, one was left with a cold and repellent puppetology. Head was a warm person who practiced a cold science, and this was also true of Luria, insofar as he practiced neuropsychology. But Luria also practiced a warm science, a "Romantic Science," as he liked to call it, heretical, secret and loving, which he practiced under the cover of an empirical, Humean science.

The "old" neurology, Head's neurology, was a science of neural mechanism and function, and, as such, descriptive and analytic, but not too therapeutic. Indeed, it is commonly said: "You neurologists, you examine, but what do you *do*?" Neurology has no answer to this—it charts impairment of mechanism and function, and hopes that time and nature may effect some sort of cure. But it is essentially a passive science.

The "new" neurology, neuropsychology, is radically different. It moved out of the Sherringtonian laboratory, with its rows of pithed and decerebrate "preparations," and into the factory, the playground, the world, where people actually do things—and it studies what they do and how they do them. Head's patients did not act, their actions were excluded; all they did was submit to passive tests. But the crucial test for neuropsychology is a test of action: A man is asked to do something—to walk, jump, skip or run—and his procedure is minutely noted. This is an absolutely radical change. Perhaps, as the noted philosopher and psychologist Richard Gregory suggests, it defines the distinction between physiology and psychology: Physiology studies mechanisms, psychology procedures. And neuropsychology studies both, but especially their relation, the working relation between mechanisms and procedures.

Although neuropsychology began with the study of "normal people," the greatest impetus to its development came from war: from the desperate need of brain- and nerve-injured soldiers for a genuine and effective neurological rehabilitation. This new science came of age, then, in Russia during World War II, and was especially the creation of the Lurias, father and son, and of Leont'ev and Zaporozhets—a galaxy of gifted and dedicated men. Neuropsychology aimed to be a science of doing, and its central concepts were those of "performance" and "procedure." As opposed to classical neurology which was essentially *static*, with its model of fixed "centers" and "functions," neuropsychology saw countless systems in continual interaction: It was essentially *dynamic*. "The organism is a unitary system," wrote Luria, and this is the credo of neuropsychology. The picture which emerges is one of a magnificent, self-activating, self-regulating automaton—and neuropsychology's founder and greatest theorist, Nicholas Bernstein, was really the founder of cybernetics, twenty years before Norbert Wiener gave it a name.

Where classical neurology rather helplessly sees "reduced function," neuropsychology identifies the affected programs and systems, and endeavors to rehabilitate by developing compensatory ones. The theoretical and practical powers, thus introduced, are immense—but, almost incredibly, this is ignored, or not known in the West. Incredibly, and quite tragically too, for we too have myriads of neurological patients, and, for the most part, we shrug our shoulders, or murmur, "Nature heals." I wish that when I myself had been a patient, such a rehabilitative program, a "neurotherapy," had been used with me. It would not only have reduced the duration of my incapacity but, equally important, would have given me the sense of being understood and the object of a genuine attempt to help. This feeling flared up with great intensity when three years after "The Leg," I read a fascinating neuropsychological book by Leont'ev and Zaporozhets

called *The Rehabilitation of the Hand*. The book affected
me so violently and personally that I immediately made a
copy of our rare library copy and covered it with passionate annotations. Unsatisfied by these marginalia, I
wrote a long essay, a critique of the book—and this is the
only time in my life I have ever done this. The book struck
home—but it also enraged me.

The facts in the "Hand" book were almost identical
to the facts in my own experience. Leont'ev and Zaporozhets studied two hundred soldiers with injured and
surgically repaired hands. Despite anatomical and neurological integrity, at least in terms of gross or classical
neurology, there was, in every case, profound distress and
incapacity. The repaired hands were "useless" and felt
"alien" to their possessors, like "objects" or "counterfeit
hands" stuck on to their wrists. Here was *my* syndrome,
exactly, multiplied by two hundred! It was clear that the
facts, the situations, the predicaments, were identical. And
to every such description—and the descriptions were very
vivid, especially if they were given in the soldiers' own
words—I wrote "Yes! Yes!"—this is exactly what had
happened to me!

What aroused my ire were the interpretations which
were given to "explain" these phenomena. For Leont'ev
and Zaporozhets, thinking in terms of systems analysis,
were apparently incapable of thinking in any other terms.
They spoke of "gnostic systems" subserving the hands,
which had become inactivated or dissociated through
injury and surgery, partly through a longish period of
forced inactivity, partly through disruption of "the afferent
field." Fair enough, very plausible—this had happened
with my leg. What puzzled and outraged me was that they

went no further—that they were satisfied, apparently, with a systems analysis, whereas their patients articulated an "existential" experience—a catastrophic change in the sense of being or body-self—vivid, powerful, and often anguished evocations of the "not real," the "not-flesh," the "not-alive," the "not-self." These descriptions were nothing short of an ontological nightmare—absolute dissolution of "identity" and "reality"—and Leont'ev and Zaporozhets could only babble on about their "gnostic systems"!

It was precisely this split which characterized Head. Head too had been given existential communications and descriptions of limbs "missing," or "feeling like cork," but could only draw diagrams and talk of "impaired function." The tendency in both cases was exactly the same—a refusal to hear or allow significance to the experiential, and an insistence on confining matters to the purely mechanical.

But what was behind this denial? The sense of "dissociation" or "alienation," to use their favorite words, was particularly strong with regard to Leont'ev and Zaporozhets, for their entire subject, their book, was *about* alienation, yet their whole aim and orientation was to deny it by interpreting it in meaningless, mechanical terms. One had the sense that a crisis was impending, that Leont'ev and Zaporozhets were close to the breaking-point, and that, sooner or later, the force of experience would burst the bounds of inadequate concepts, of mechanicalness, of empiricism itself . . . as such a breakthrough had happened with me.

But there was something very strange, beyond the bounds of mere resistance here. For Leont'ev and Zaporozhets not only dwelt on the phenomena, but used rather striking language to describe it: They spoke of patients being "blind" and "deaf" to their own hands. *Yet they themselves were blind and deaf to the elemental implications of such "blindness" and "deafness."* What they describe, without realizing it, is a perceptual blind spot, a scotoma, in their patients; but they fail to realize it because of their own conceptual blind spot. This intellectual scotoma, at the very center of their formulations and thoughts, is characteristic of all neuropsychology which deals with systems but ignores the self. What Leont'ev and Zaporozhets "scotomize" unwittingly is precisely the center, the living self, of their patients. And it was this which outraged me and made me realize that neuropsychology, though it deals with performances and procedures, is, at heart, still a puppetology.

How could they be so blind, how could they not see?—and then I thought of how blind I too had been. And yet Leont'ev and Zaporozhets understood that activity was the essence of rehabilitation: The patient is "tricked" into using the inactive limb, and the moment this happens, the alienation is gone, and the limb returns to its owner, in full and glorious reality and vitality. This understanding afforded me extreme delight. "Yes! Yes!" I exclaimed excitedly in the margin. "This was exactly how it happened with me!" But then I got furious, when Leont'ev and Zaporozhets presumed to "analyze" their findings. What they describe, with great fidelity, is the fact, the phenomenon, the power, of *spontaneity*. Preparations might be made, indeed must be made—but the actual act, when it occurs, is a spontaneous event: as spontaneous as my swimming when I was thrown into the pool, as spontaneous as my walking when Mendelssohn "played." They describe it, and then they do not "see" it: for they insist on analyzing it in mechanical terms. They speak of "programs," "procedures," "solving the motor task"—as if their patients were computers, or "cyborgs." They miss the essential beauty and mystery of action, they miss its grace, its musicality. They miss the very sense of movement. And it was this, just this, which had to be regained.

And now, I realized, after a long hour of stasis, we had emerged from the siding, and we were moving again.

Leont'ev and Zaporozhets' book, read just after Luria's death, provoked a sort of crisis in me. I had, somehow, in the insistence and indulgence of denial, managed to disavow my own thoughts and observations, to see them as eccentric, to doubt their importance. But these phenomena, which I doubted when they occurred in me, were beyond doubt when I saw them in Leont'ev and Zaporozhets. Here were hundreds of observations identical with my own— deprived of all importance by the inadequate theory which went with them.

When Luria died, I wrote an obituary for *The Times*, in which, by implication, I compared him to Hume. I loved, admired, and trusted him, as I had Hume; and now I felt dissatisfied with him, as I had felt dissatisfied with Hume.

As long as Luria was alive, I admitted only the positive feelings, not the secret dissatisfaction which went along with them. With his death, there was both grief and liberation. Now I could accept that one had to go beyond Luria, as he had gone beyond his own "fathers" and teachers. I felt in this the propriety of tradition, by which each generation of thought gives way to the next. But this gentle vision was shattered by Leont'ev, who outraged me and brought about reaction and crisis.

These are not feelings which are easy to admit. Einstein, writing in *The Evolution of Physics*, and speaking of "The Downfall of the Mechanical View," beguiles us with a gentle and endearing image: ". . . creating a new theory is not like destroying an old barn and erecting a skyscraper in its place. It is rather like climbing a mountain, gaining new and wider views. . . . But the point from which we started still exists. . . ."

In giving us this image, Einstein manages to pay graceful tribute to his fathers and forebears, and to conceal the violent gap which Revolution—unlike Evolution—entails, that great and frightening gap between the old and the new, when the past is no longer, and the future is not yet. This explains why Moses Mendelssohn called Kant the "all-destroyer," the *alles Zermelmer*. And why Wittgenstein, after feeling that his original philosophy, the *Tractatus*, had collapsed "like a house of cards," spent several years in intellectual darkness before his new philosophy came to birth.

Such a darkness came on me after reading Leont'ev; and I wondered if I would ever emerge from it. Neuropsychology had crashed in ruins about me—it retained all of its practical uses and powers, but it had lost all its promise of anything deeper. And if empirical science had failed me as a guide to the musicality of action and life, so too did Hume and the philosophy of empiricism, of which empirical science was founded.

The darkness was full of fear, but it had beauty too—for, from the darkness, I dared hope, there would come a new light. Had I been religious I would have called it the "Darkness of God."

"The years of searching in the dark for a truth one feels but cannot express . . ."

Such were the years that followed "The Leg," and the darkness was exacerbated on reading "The Hand." Neuropsychology—the science of robotics—could not begin to explain the climax of my experience, the sudden sense of being a living and free agent, and not a mere robot struggling with motor tasks. It could not prepare me for the sudden sense of delight and spontaneity, which came to me, as from heaven, the moment the Mendelssohn came. It could cast no light on the nature of the *experience*, or on the *experiencer*, myself; it could cast no light on the nature of *action*, or on the *actor*, myself. The experiencing, acting subject was wholly denied—as it is in empirical science, in Hume.

"I venture to affirm," Hume writes, ". . . that [we] are nothing but a bundle or collection of different perceptions, succeeding one another with inconceivable rapidity, and in a perceptual flux and movement."

But there is nothing *behind* these perceptions, this flux and movement—there is no experiencer, no actor, no *person* at all. This is Hume's conclusion, as it is the conclusion of empirical science, of any purely "objective" approach: And it is utterly at odds with all our deepest feelings, that we *do* experience, and act, and exist. What I felt so intensely, in these two years of dark, was a need to assert and affirm the living subject, to escape from a purely objective, or "robotic," science, to find and establish what was missing—a living "I." If Sherringtonian neurology was the study of "trigger puppets," and Lurian neurology the study of self-activating robots, I had to go beyond these to *a neurology of the soul*.

Years ago I spoke to Auden about my "mechanical" Parkinsonians, showed him some motion pictures, asked what was "missing."

"Music," he exclaimed, without hesitation. "The music of motion. This is what they lack, this is what they need," and he instantly quoted an aphorism of Novalis': "Every disease is a musical problem, every cure a musical solution."

". . . I don't know if this is so of *every* disease," he added, "but it is certainly, spectacularly, the case here. Novalis might have been thinking of your patients!"

He wondered whether music might "work" for a Parkinsonian, restore him, while it lasted, to a free and normal action.

Yes, music could "center" my patients. And, as I was to find, it had equal power, an elemental power, with *every* patient, restoring the inner music, the "musical" self, which had been lost through neurological injury or disease.

Following practice came formulation: I constantly spoke of "centering" the patient, finding and evoking a living personal center, an "I," amid the debris of neurological devastation.

This had been my practice, my language, for many years—what I knew, from experience, to be essential for patients. But I had no philosophical backing for this knowledge, no system of concepts into which it would fit. It was only when I came to read Kant that I found this conceptual and philosophical backing. Kant *vindicated* what I had learned with my patients. Kant was the light.

In Kant, then, I found, first, *living* concepts of space and time—space and time as they articulated life, and allowed the organization of a living stream of experience and action. Kant restored what Hume had removed, the center, the concept of self—the self as the center of experience and action. Further, I found in Kant the concept of "freedom," that freedom without which the grace of animal motion is impossible. Kant understood the leap from succession to stream, from position to posture, from mechanism to grace, which the accession of life involved. All of this had rushed on me without my understanding it in the moment of my first "Mendelssohnian" walk. Suddenly, in reading Kant, I not only understood what my own experience had been about, had *meant*, but what the experiences of countless patients I had seen had been about as well—I understood where a proper neurology, a neurological medicine, should go.

William James dreamed of "A higher and simpler way of looking at Nature," which we may hope one day to reach or return to. This, I felt, was what Kant was about, what he promised, when one finally came to him. Enriched with the spoils of analytical science, one might now, armed with

Kant, soar up to that "higher and simpler" viewpoint which James dreamed of.

This was what I myself had felt, or obscurely dreamed, eight years before, when I had recovered, as by a miracle, my full and free self, and wandered up onto Parliament Hill, dreaming of a new science, "a new field."

Now, as my train neared its destination, after a day-long journey wrapped in reading and thought, reliving the experiences and thoughts of many years, I felt an immense gratitude, a deep peace stealing upon me.

The human science, the human medicine, I had glimpsed years before had rooted itself, deeper and deeper, within me, calling equally to the depths of heart and mind. And it was not just a new "field" or even a new science that opened to me, but a new and wholly delightful sphere of life and mind. The frightful, frightening lines in *Faust* had proved wrong: there need not be a gulf, or a split, between joyous life and grey theory—but, on the contrary, a wonderful coming together.

As a child I loved nothing more than stories of naturalists and scientific exploration—Darwin on the *Beagle*, Bates on the Amazon. I had always dreamed that I too might go on such a voyage, travel to and explore far-off places. And now, I realized, sitting in a train drawing into Grand Central Station, this was neither more nor less than I had done. There had not, perhaps, been much physical movement; but sitting in hospital, first as patient, then as doctor, I had travelled as far, as strangely, as my heart could desire, had seen and explored a whole new world of thought: ". . . he, who for decades instead of speculating concerning a new Atlantis had really wandered in the trackless wilds of a new continent and undertaken bits of virgin cultivation. . . ."

Yes, I dared apply Husserl's word to myself. I had indeed found "a new field," and had wandered in the "trackless wilds of a new continent." I dared believe, further, in Husserl's words, that I had seen "the far horizons, the structural formations, of an infinite open country," of a new and true way of thinking.

But what was important was not that I "saw" it, but that there *was* a "there"—a wonderful continent, a infinite open country, a new realm, to which the neurology and medicine of the future might aspire.

I dreamed this as a child; and, more clearly, on Hampstead Heath; and now, with a still greater sense of its possibility and reality, I gazed at the bright and warm vision of "the promised land," tucked the two bulky volumes under my arm, and walked into the November night.